Disclosures

Contents

Introduction: A Scoop of Inspiration

Riley Harris was no ordinary teenager. She walked the bustling halls of John Bowne High School with a purpose and passion that few of her classmates understood. While her friends worried about trending outfits, social media posts, and weekend plans, Riley was a quiet storm of ideas, ambition, and a deep desire to create something of her own. Growing up as the only child of Ron and Cynthia Harris, a hard-working couple in the heart of Queens, New York, she knew what it meant to appreciate small things and dream big.

Her parents raised her with a deep appreciation for creativity, resilience, and authenticity. They weren't rich, but they provided Riley with a solid foundation, encouraging her natural curiosity and independence. So when Ron and Cynthia surprised her with a summer family trip to Paris, Riley had no idea that it would spark a life-changing adventure and set her on a path she'd only ever dreamed of.

This is the story of how a single taste of something extraordinary could ignite a passion, and how one determined teenager from Queens became known as "The Ice Cream Girl from Queens," capturing the hearts (and taste buds) of people. Riley's story is one of inspiration, resilience, and the power of following one's dreams — one scoop at a time.

Chapter 1: The Dreamer in Queens

Riley Harris leaned against the window of her small bedroom, gazing down at the bustling street of Queens that stretched out beneath her. The sounds were all so familiar—the honking horns, the shouts of street vendors setting up for the day, the distant rumble of the subway. Even on the quietest of mornings, Queens had its own rhythm, a constant hum that filled the air. The buildings, tall and crammed side by side, were like old friends she knew by heart, each one holding stories, laughter, and the many faces she saw daily. She loved this place with all its quirks and flaws, but somehow, she always felt as though she belonged somewhere else too.

At fifteen, Riley was just beginning to understand her own dreams and ambitions, but they felt big, vast, and uncontained, sometimes even too big for Queens. She often wondered if her aspirations were like helium balloons, rising higher than she could reach. Her sophomore year at John Bowne High School was a constant mix of excitement and longing. She had friends she cared about deeply, people she laughed with at lunch, shared secrets with, and whose company brought her comfort. Still, there was a quiet corner in her heart that her friends couldn't reach, a place filled with dreams they might not understand.

As she walked the halls of John Bowne, she would sometimes find herself lost in thought, a habit her friends teased her about. Riley, they'd say, was always in her head, living in some far-off world while they were busy talking about the latest fashion trends, new songs, or the TikTok dances everyone was trying to learn. It wasn't that Riley didn't enjoy those things, but she wanted more. She wanted to create something all her own, something beautiful and meaningful that could outlast the fleeting trends of the world around her.

Her notebooks were filled with sketches, ideas for art projects, and fragments of poems she'd jot down between classes. Some were just scribbles, half-formed thoughts that she wasn't ready to share with anyone. But others...others were the beginnings of something bigger, pieces of a puzzle she was slowly putting together. She knew that one day, these scattered ideas might lead her somewhere new, somewhere beyond Queens. Her friends liked to call her the "dreamer," and while they meant it with affection, Riley sometimes wondered if they really understood what that meant for her.

At home, her parents were her biggest supporters, even if they didn't fully grasp the scope of her dreams. Ron and Cynthia Harris were simple, hardworking people. Ron was a mechanic, his hands always rough and stained with grease, while Cynthia worked as a receptionist at a dental clinic, her smile warm and welcoming to everyone she met. They weren't wealthy by any means, but they had always provided Riley with a life rich in love, laughter, and encouragement. She knew how lucky she was to have them, and their small, cozy apartment felt like a haven, a place where she could dream freely without judgment.

Every evening, the three of them gathered around their worn wooden dining table for dinner, a ritual that felt almost sacred in its simplicity. They would share stories from their day, each taking turns as they passed around bowls of pasta or platters of roasted vegetables. Ron would tell funny stories about his clients and the cars he fixed, giving each vehicle a personality as if they were characters in a novel. Cynthia would add her own anecdotes, sharing humorous moments from the dental clinic that had everyone laughing.

Riley loved these moments, the warmth of their home, the feeling of being completely understood and loved. But even as she sat at the table, laughing with her parents, a part of her felt restless, a flicker of longing she couldn't quite explain. It was as though she were waiting for something to happen, something that would show her where she truly belonged.

One evening, as they were finishing up dinner, her father set down his fork, looking at Riley with a glint of excitement in his eyes. "Riley, your mom and I have been planning a little surprise for you," he said, glancing at Cynthia, who was barely able to contain her smile. Riley looked back and forth between them, her curiosity piqued.

"What kind of surprise?" she asked, leaning forward eagerly.

Cynthia reached across the table, taking Riley's hand in hers. "How would you feel about going to Paris this summer?"

For a moment, Riley just stared at her, unsure if she had heard correctly. Paris? The city of lights, art, and romance, a place she had dreamed of but never imagined she'd actually see. She had read about it in books, seen it in movies, and pictured herself walking along the Seine, exploring the museums, and standing beneath the Eiffel Tower. But to actually go? It felt like a dream too good to be true.

"Are you serious?" she whispered, her eyes wide with disbelief.

Ron chuckled, nodding. "We've been saving up for a while now, and we wanted to do something special for you. You work so hard, Riley, and we thought Paris might be the inspiration you're looking for."

Riley threw her arms around her parents, overwhelmed with gratitude and excitement. She could hardly believe it. Paris! Her mind raced with possibilities, imagining all the places she'd see, the art she'd study, the food she'd taste. It felt like the door to another world had just opened, and she was ready to step through it.

In the weeks leading up to the trip, Riley's anticipation grew with each passing day. She read everything she could about Paris, filling her sketchbook with drawings of the Eiffel Tower, the Louvre, and the charming cafés she dreamed of visiting. She practiced French phrases in front of the mirror, laughing at her own attempts as she stumbled through "Bonjour," "Merci," and "Où est le musée?" She created her own itinerary, jotting down the names of hidden art galleries, pastry shops, and quiet gardens she hoped to explore.

The night before their departure, Riley could hardly sleep, her mind buzzing with excitement. She imagined herself walking through Paris, surrounded by the rich history and beauty she had read about. She thought of the artists who had come before her, those who had wandered the same streets, found inspiration in the same landscapes, and created works that had stood the test of time. She wanted to be part of that legacy, even if she didn't yet know how.

When the morning finally arrived, Riley and her parents piled into a cab, their suitcases stacked beside them as they headed to the airport. The city flashed by outside the window, and Riley felt a pang of sadness, realizing that she would miss Queens even though she was about to embark on the adventure of a lifetime. Her parents were just as excited, grinning from ear to ear as they checked in and made their way through security.

On the plane, Riley settled into her seat, her heart pounding with a mixture of excitement and nerves. She spent most of the flight staring out the window, watching as the familiar landscape of New York faded into a sea of clouds. She was heading toward a place she had only dreamed of, a place that held promises of inspiration and possibility.

As they descended into Paris, Riley felt a rush of exhilaration. The city stretched out below them, a tapestry of rooftops, winding streets, and sparkling rivers. She pressed her face to the window, barely able to contain her excitement as the plane touched down. This was it. She was in Paris, the city that had fueled her dreams for so long.

As they stepped out of the airport, Riley was immediately struck by the difference in the air. It smelled of fresh bread and flowers, a faint hint of perfume drifting from the crowd of people around them. The signs were all in French, and the sound of the language filled the air, musical and elegant. It was like stepping into another world, a place that felt both foreign and strangely familiar.

They took a cab to their hotel, and Riley couldn't take her eyes off the city that unfolded before her. The buildings were tall and majestic, each one with its own character and charm. Wrought-iron balconies lined the windows, flowers spilling over the edges in bursts of color. She spotted bakeries, cafés, and bookstores on nearly every corner, each one a temptation she was eager to explore.

Their hotel was a charming little place nestled in a quiet neighborhood, with ivy climbing the stone walls and a view of a quaint square. Riley felt like she had stepped into a painting, the kind she had studied in art class. Everything was beautiful, down to the smallest detail, and she felt a surge of gratitude for this incredible opportunity.

Chapter 2: Paris Awakening

Riley could hardly sleep that night. Her mind was buzzing with the sights, sounds, and flavors she'd experienced during her first day in Paris. It was unlike anything she'd ever known—a sensory whirlwind that left her both exhilarated and exhausted. She lay awake in her small hotel bed, listening to the muffled sounds of the city outside, feeling a thrill each time she remembered that she was here, in Paris, a place that had once only existed in her dreams.

As the first rays of sunlight peeked through her window, Riley was already wide awake, eager to explore. She tiptoed around the room, careful not to wake her parents as she dressed and slipped on her shoes. She had always been an early riser, someone who found peace in the quiet moments of dawn. But here, in a city as old and storied as Paris, the morning felt magical, a secret she was privileged to witness.

Riley stepped outside and was immediately greeted by the crisp morning air, cool and fresh with the faint scent of flowers from a nearby florist. The streets were quieter than she'd expected, with only a few Parisians going about their early-morning routines. She wandered along the cobblestone streets, her eyes wide as she took in the details that made this city feel so alive—the wrought-iron balconies with flower boxes spilling over, the elegant streetlamps that seemed to belong to another era, and the quiet elegance of the buildings, each one bearing the weight of centuries.

As she strolled, Riley couldn't help but marvel at how different everything felt from her neighborhood in Queens. There, the mornings were busy, noisy, and vibrant in their own way, but here, there was a kind of poetry in the silence, a beauty that spoke to her in a language she couldn't quite understand but longed to know.

By the time her parents woke up and joined her for breakfast at a nearby café, Riley had already filled several pages of her sketchbook with drawings and notes. She wanted to capture every detail, every emotion, as if preserving them on paper would allow her to carry a piece of Paris back with her.

Their days in Paris quickly fell into a rhythm of exploration and discovery. They would start with breakfast at a different café each morning, where Riley savored every flaky, buttery bite of croissant, each sip of rich, dark coffee. The pastries were like nothing she had tasted back home—delicate, intricate, and bursting with flavor. She felt as though each one was a work of art, crafted with the same care and attention to detail as the paintings that filled the city's museums.

The mornings were usually spent wandering through the iconic landmarks. They visited the Eiffel Tower, where Riley was struck by the sheer scale of the structure, its iron latticework rising high above the city. She couldn't help but wonder about the countless artists and dreamers who had stood in the same spot, gazing up at the tower and feeling that same sense of awe.

The Louvre was another revelation. Riley had always loved art, but seeing these masterpieces in person was a completely different experience. She wandered through the galleries, her gaze lingering on the Mona Lisa's enigmatic smile, the delicate lines of the Venus de Milo, the intense colors of Delacroix's *Liberty Leading the People*. Each painting, each sculpture, felt like a story waiting to be told, a piece of history preserved in brushstrokes and marble.

Riley's sketchbook quickly filled with her impressions of these artworks, rough sketches of the scenes she saw, and notes on the colors and textures that spoke to her. She was inspired in a way she hadn't felt before, a spark ignited by the beauty and depth of the art surrounding her.

But it was the quieter moments, away from the famous landmarks, that seemed to touch her most deeply. One afternoon, her parents decided to rest back at the hotel, and Riley took the opportunity to explore on her own. She found herself wandering down a narrow side street, lined with tiny shops and cafés, each one with its own unique character. The scent of fresh bread and pastries wafted through the air, mingling with the faint aroma of coffee and lavender from a nearby florist.

As she rounded a corner, she spotted a small, unassuming ice cream shop with a wooden sign that read *Glace Fermière*. The name caught her attention; she knew that "glace" meant ice cream in French, but she was unfamiliar with "fermière." Curious, she stepped inside, feeling as though she were crossing a threshold into another world.

The shop was small and cozy, with rustic wooden shelves lined with jars of ingredients, each labeled in elegant French script. Photographs of farms and orchards decorated the walls, images of cows grazing in sunlit fields, baskets of fresh fruit, and farmers working in lush green fields. It was nothing like the brightly lit, bustling ice cream parlors she was used to in New York. Here, there was a sense of peace, a quiet reverence for the ingredients and the craft of making ice cream.

The woman behind the counter greeted her with a warm smile and a gentle "Bonjour." Riley returned the greeting, feeling a rush of pride at her ability to use the few words of French she'd learned. The woman began to explain, in a mix of French and English, that their ice cream was called "glace fermière," meaning it was made with ingredients directly sourced from farms. The milk came from cows raised on local farms, the fruit was harvested by hand, and each batch of ice cream was crafted with care and precision, preserving the natural flavors.

Riley listened, captivated, as the woman described the philosophy behind glace fermière. It was about honoring the land, respecting the animals, and celebrating the richness of nature. This wasn't just ice cream; it was a connection to the earth, a story told through taste.

She ordered a scoop of caramel vanilla, and as she took her first bite, she felt a wave of sensation wash over her. The ice cream was rich and creamy, the caramel dark and smoky, balanced perfectly by the light sweetness of the vanilla. She closed her eyes, savoring each flavor as it unfolded on her tongue, feeling as though she were tasting ice cream for the very first time.

Riley returned to *Glace Fermière* every day after that, eager to try new flavors and learn more about the shop's unique approach to ice cream. She sampled flavors like lavender honey, which tasted like a summer garden in bloom; fig, sweet and earthy; and chestnut, rich and warm with a hint of nuttiness. Each one was a revelation, a new experience that opened her eyes to the possibilities of flavor.

The shopkeeper explained that each flavor was carefully crafted to highlight the natural ingredients, with no artificial colors or preservatives. They used seasonal fruits, local honey, and fresh herbs to create ice creams that celebrated the beauty of nature. Riley was fascinated by the attention to detail, the dedication to quality, and the respect for tradition that went into each scoop.

As the days went by, Riley found herself thinking more and more about the idea of bringing this kind of ice cream back to New York. She imagined opening her own shop, a place where people could experience the same joy and wonder she felt with each bite. She dreamed of introducing her friends, her family, her whole neighborhood to the flavors and philosophy she had discovered here in Paris.

One afternoon, as she sat on a bench outside the shop, enjoying a scoop of lavender honey ice cream, Riley felt a sense of clarity she hadn't known before. This wasn't just a passing idea—it was a vision, a calling. She wanted to create something that would bring people the same happiness she felt in that moment, something that would connect them to the land, to each other, and to the beauty of simple, natural flavors.

The thought of starting a business at fifteen was daunting, and she had no idea where to even begin. But as she looked around at the quaint shop, the people passing by with smiles on their faces, she felt a spark of determination. She didn't need to have all the answers right now; she just needed to believe in her vision and take it one step at a time.

On their final day in Paris, Riley returned to *Glace Fermière* one last time, savoring her favorite flavor—caramel vanilla—as she took in every detail of the shop, committing it to memory. She wanted to remember this place, the feeling it gave her, and the dreams it had inspired.

As they boarded the plane back to New York, Riley was filled with a sense of excitement and purpose she had never felt before. She knew that her life was about to change, that this trip to Paris had given her more than just memories; it had given her a vision for her future.

As the plane lifted off, she looked out the window at the city below, feeling a mixture of gratitude and sadness. Paris had given her something precious, something she would carry with her forever. She didn't know how or when, but she was determined to bring a piece of Paris back to Queens, to share the magic of glace fermière with the people she loved.

When they landed in New York, Riley felt like a different person. She had come to Paris as a dreamer, a girl with a love for art and adventure, but she was returning home with a purpose, a plan. She didn't have all the answers, but she had a vision, a spark that would guide her as she began this new chapter of her life.

Riley took a deep breath, feeling the familiar pulse of Queens as they stepped out of the airport and into the city. She was home, but she knew that things would never be the same. The adventure was just beginning, and she was ready to follow her dreams, wherever they might lead.

Chapter 3: The Big Idea

Returning home to Queens, Riley found herself with a new kind of energy, one that had her mind buzzing with thoughts and ideas that wouldn't stop. Paris had left her with more than just memories; it had gifted her a dream she could almost taste, a vision she was determined to bring to life. She could see it now—a small, charming shop in her neighborhood, one that echoed the authenticity of the little ice cream shop she'd discovered on the streets of Paris. Riley was home, but her heart was still lingering in the quiet, sweet world of *glace fermière*, and she couldn't shake the feeling that this was something she was meant to create.

Each day after school, Riley would retreat to her room, her mind still buzzing from her trip and the idea that was now consuming her thoughts. She found herself drawn to her notebook, flipping through the pages filled with sketches, ideas, and half-formed plans she had scribbled during her time in Paris. It was as though each page whispered to her, urging her to pursue this dream, to turn these sketches into something real. She could practically see the shop—its cozy wooden shelves, the jars of ingredients, the photos of farms lining the walls. It was a dream that felt just within her grasp, yet she knew it would take everything she had to make it happen.

Her nights became dedicated to research, hours spent online as she tried to learn everything she could about French ice cream, *glace fermière*, and the art of making artisanal ice cream. She started with the basics, reading about the history of French ice cream, how it was different from American styles, and the unique ingredients and techniques that set it apart. She learned that *glace* had a creamier texture, often made with a custard base that used more egg yolks than typical American ice creams. This gave it a richness and depth of flavor that she had fallen in love with during her time in Paris.

But Riley didn't stop there. She began to delve into the world of organic farming, curious about how the ingredients in *glace fermière* were sourced. She read about sustainable dairy practices, small family farms that prioritized the health of their animals and the quality of their products. The idea of using milk from cows that roamed freely on open pastures, eating natural grasses, fascinated her. It felt like a piece of the puzzle, something essential to the quality and authenticity she wanted to bring to her own ice cream.

As her research deepened, Riley found herself taking notes on everything she learned, her notebook now filled with facts and figures, ideas for flavors, and sketches of the shop she dreamed of. She even jotted down potential names, experimenting with words and phrases that captured the essence of her vision. Each idea felt like a step closer to making her dream a reality, and she found herself becoming more and more attached to the thought of creating something truly special.

During dinner, Riley would share her latest discoveries with her parents, her excitement barely contained as she told them about the differences between American and French ice cream, the importance of high-quality ingredients, and the concept of farm-to-table production. Cynthia and Ron listened with amused interest, exchanging glances as their daughter spoke with a passion they hadn't seen in her before. They could see how much this dream meant to her, how deeply she believed in the idea, even if it sounded a bit far-fetched.

Cynthia would nod along, her eyes warm with encouragement, while Ron leaned back in his chair, arms crossed, a thoughtful expression on his face. He was proud of his daughter's ambition, but he also knew the reality of hard work and the challenges that lay ahead. Still, he couldn't help but be impressed by her dedication, her willingness to dive into something so unfamiliar with such determination.

Riley's friends, however, didn't share her enthusiasm. When she tried to explain her dream, to tell them about the magic of *glace fermière* and her plan to create a farm-to-table ice cream shop in Queens, they mostly laughed it off. To them, it seemed like just another one of Riley's quirky ideas, something she would eventually move on from. They didn't understand the depth of her passion, the way this idea had taken root in her heart and wouldn't let go.

It hurt, even though Riley tried to brush it off. She had hoped they would see what she saw, feel the excitement that had gripped her ever since she'd first tasted that caramel vanilla ice cream in Paris. But instead, they treated it as a passing hobby, something fun but ultimately unimportant. Riley found herself pulling away, spending more time on her own, focused on her dream and determined to prove to herself— and to them—that this was more than just a fleeting fancy.

Her parents noticed the shift, the way Riley seemed quieter, more withdrawn, but they didn't push. They could see that she was working through something, that this dream was both a source of excitement and a challenge she was trying to navigate. Cynthia would find her daughter in her room, surrounded by books and notebooks, her face focused and serious as she jotted down notes or sketched ideas. Ron would catch glimpses of her in the kitchen, experimenting with flavors, her face lighting up whenever she discovered something new.

One evening, after another conversation about her research, Ron looked at Riley, a glint of pride in his eyes. "You know, Riley," he said, "if you really want to pursue this, maybe it's time to take the next step."

Riley's heart skipped a beat. "The next step?"

"Research is great," Cynthia added, "but maybe it's time you see how these things actually work. Talk to some people who are already doing this."

Her parents' words sparked something in Riley, a realization that if she wanted to make this dream a reality, she needed more than just research and ideas. She needed experience, guidance, someone who understood the world of organic farming and could show her what it really took to create something from the ground up. It was then that an idea came to her—Amish country.

She remembered reading about the Amish and their dedication to traditional farming methods, their commitment to organic practices and high-quality dairy products. It sounded exactly like what she wanted, a place where she could learn about farm-to-table production and maybe even find a partner who shared her values.

But convincing her parents to take a trip to Amish country was no small feat. She knew they supported her dream, but a trip like this would require planning, time, and a bit of persuasion. Riley spent the next few days preparing her case, gathering everything she had learned about Amish farming practices, the importance of high-quality dairy, and how this experience could help her understand the realities of her dream.

When she finally sat down with her parents, she presented her case as though she were pitching a business idea. She spoke with conviction, explaining the benefits of organic, sustainable farming and how it would contribute to the quality of her ice cream. She told them about the Amish commitment to natural methods, the way their cows were raised, and the care they put into their products. By the time she finished, Cynthia and Ron were nodding, impressed by her dedication and the thoughtfulness of her plan.

"We can go this weekend," Ron said, a hint of pride in his voice. "I think it's time we see what this dream of yours is all about."

Riley felt a surge of excitement, a mix of gratitude and anticipation that left her speechless. She hugged her parents, barely able to contain her joy. This was it—the first real step toward making her dream a reality.

That week was a blur of preparation, as Riley planned out their trip, researched the farms she wanted to visit, and made a list of questions she hoped to ask. She felt like a young entrepreneur, someone on the brink of something extraordinary. She could hardly wait to see Amish country, to meet the people who could help her turn her vision into something tangible.

By the time the weekend arrived, Riley was ready, her heart full of hope and determination. She had a vision, a plan, and now, with her parents by her side, she was taking her first step toward bringing her dream to life.

Chapter 4: A Visit to Amish Country

The morning of their trip to Amish country dawned bright and clear, and Riley could barely contain her excitement. She had spent the past few days preparing, making a list of everything she wanted to ask and learn, and she had even packed her notebook filled with sketches and notes from her Paris experience. This trip felt like the next crucial step, a chance to connect with people who could help her make her farm-to-table ice cream dream a reality. As she waited for her parents to get ready, she stood by the window, her gaze fixed on the city skyline as it glittered in the morning sun. The busy streets of Queens had been her entire world for as long as she could remember, but today, she was venturing into something completely new.

The drive out of the city was long, the scenery changing gradually from the dense, bustling streets of New York to the open, rolling countryside of Pennsylvania. As the buildings gave way to fields, Riley felt a sense of calm settle over her. The fields stretched endlessly on either side of the road, lush and green, dotted with barns, silos, and the occasional farmhouse. It was a landscape she had rarely seen, and each mile seemed to take her further from the familiar world she knew.

Her father, Ron, drove with steady focus, his hands gripping the wheel as he navigated the winding country roads. Riley could sense his quiet pride, the way he glanced at her in the rearview mirror with a look that said he was impressed by her determination. Her mother, Cynthia, sat beside him, turning around every so often to chat with Riley, asking her about the farms they were planning to visit and what she hoped to learn.

They reached the Amish community by late morning, passing horse-drawn buggies on the road and small farms surrounded by wooden fences. Everything seemed simpler here, slower and more intentional. Riley felt a deep sense of respect for the people who lived this way, dedicating themselves to a life of simplicity and hard work.

Their first stop was a small, family-owned dairy farm, where Riley had arranged to meet a man named Mr. Stoltzfus. He was known in the community for his commitment to organic farming practices and the high quality of his dairy products. As they pulled into the gravel driveway, Riley took a deep breath, trying to steady the nervous excitement that had been building inside her. This was her chance to learn from someone who understood the values she wanted to build her business on.

The farm was beautiful in its simplicity. A large red barn stood at the center of the property, flanked by open pastures where cows grazed lazily in the sun. Chickens roamed freely near the barn, clucking softly as they pecked at the ground, and a few children ran across the yard, laughing as they chased each other in circles. Riley felt a sense of peace wash over her as she took in the scene, the quiet beauty of a life connected to the land.

Mr. Stoltzfus greeted them at the entrance to the barn, his handshake firm and warm. He was a tall, lean man with a weathered face and kind eyes, his clothes simple and practical, reflecting the values of his community. Riley immediately felt at ease in his presence, sensing his sincerity and his dedication to his work.

They began with a tour of the farm, Mr. Stoltzfus explaining each aspect of his operation with a gentle pride. He spoke about the cows with a tenderness that surprised Riley, describing how they were raised on pasture, free to graze on the natural grasses that grew in the fields. "Our cows are like family," he said with a smile. "We take care of them, and in return, they give us milk of the highest quality. It's a partnership, you could say."

Riley listened intently, her heart swelling with admiration for the man and his philosophy. She asked him about his farming methods, curious about everything from the type of grass the cows ate to the way the milk was processed. Mr. Stoltzfus explained that everything on the farm was done with care and intention, from the feeding and milking of the cows to the storage of the milk. Nothing was rushed, and nothing was wasted. It was a stark contrast to the commercial dairy farms she had read about, where efficiency often took precedence over quality.

They walked through the barn, where Riley saw the milking stations and the storage tanks where the milk was kept before being transported to the local market. The smell of hay and fresh milk filled the air, mingling with the earthy scent of the animals. It was a sensory experience unlike any she had known, grounding her in the reality of where her ingredients would come from if she pursued this path.

Riley's mind was spinning with ideas and questions, her notebook quickly filling with notes as she scribbled down everything Mr. Stoltzfus said. She asked about his thoughts on organic certification, curious about the challenges he faced in maintaining his standards without the use of chemicals or artificial additives. He explained that organic farming was a labor of love, a commitment to respecting the land and the animals, even when it was difficult or costly.

She felt a profound sense of respect for his dedication and found herself more determined than ever to honor these principles in her own business. The more she learned, the clearer her vision became. She wanted her ice cream to reflect the same values, to be a product that was both delicious and ethically made, something that connected people to the land in a way that was rare and special.

After the tour, they sat together on the porch of the farmhouse, the air filled with the soft sounds of the farm—the lowing of cows, the rustle of leaves, and the occasional cluck of a chicken. Riley felt a deep sense of peace, a feeling of being exactly where she was meant to be. She shared her vision with Mr. Stoltzfus, explaining her dream of creating a farm-to-table ice cream business that would capture the essence of *glace fermière*.

Mr. Stoltzfus listened with a thoughtful expression, nodding as she spoke. When she finished, he looked at her with a gentle smile. "It's not often I meet someone your age with such a clear sense of purpose," he said. "You remind me of myself when I was young, eager to create something meaningful."

They discussed the logistics of a partnership, talking about the quantities of milk she would need, the timing of deliveries, and the costs involved. Mr. Stoltzfus offered advice on how to scale production without compromising quality, sharing his own experiences and the lessons he had learned over the years. He was patient and generous with his knowledge, answering each of Riley's questions with a calm assurance that reassured her.

By the end of their conversation, they had reached an agreement. Mr. Stoltzfus would supply her with the dairy she needed to begin her first batches of ice cream, and Riley promised to uphold the values he had instilled in her during their time together. She would create a product that honored his hard work, a tribute to the quality and care that went into every drop of milk.

As they prepared to leave, Riley felt a deep sense of gratitude, not only for the partnership they had formed but for the opportunity to learn from someone who shared her vision. She hugged Mr. Stoltzfus, thanking him for his generosity and his belief in her dream. He smiled, patting her shoulder with a nod. "You're welcome back anytime," he said. "Remember, building something worthwhile takes patience and perseverance. But with your passion, I have no doubt you'll succeed."

The drive back to Queens was filled with excited conversation, Riley sharing every detail of the farm visit with her parents. She spoke about the cows, the fields, the philosophy of organic farming, her words spilling out in a rush of enthusiasm. Cynthia and Ron listened, smiling as they saw the light in her eyes, the confidence that had blossomed during her time on the farm.

When they finally arrived home, Riley couldn't wait to get started. She felt like she was on the brink of something extraordinary, a journey that would lead her from the quiet fields of Amish country to the bustling streets of Queens, connecting two worlds through the simple pleasure of ice cream. She knew the path ahead would be challenging, filled with obstacles she couldn't yet foresee, but she felt ready, her heart and mind united in a single purpose.

That night, as she lay in bed, Riley's mind was filled with thoughts of the farm, the cows grazing peacefully in the fields, and the steady presence of Mr. Stoltzfus, a man whose dedication to quality and integrity had inspired her in ways she hadn't expected. She drifted off to sleep with a sense of peace and determination, knowing that her dream was no longer just an idea but a reality she was building, one step at a time.

Chapter 5: First Batch, First Taste Test

Riley's kitchen was a whirlwind of activity. Her countertops, usually reserved for family meals, were now transformed into a bustling workspace. Bowls, spoons, jars of ingredients, and her carefully penned notes were scattered across every available surface. She was finally ready to embark on her first batch of ice cream, and she was filled with an anticipation that seemed to electrify the air around her.

Everything she had prepared was centered around authenticity—the concept that had captured her heart in Paris. And thanks to Mr. Stoltzfus, her dream was anchored by ingredients that went beyond just quality; they embodied the very essence of farm-to-table. His farm supplied her with the dairy, rich and unprocessed, as well as other essentials that had been harvested with care. Mr. Stoltzfus had even provided raw honey, a product from his own hives, a gift Riley hadn't expected but one that felt like a perfect addition. Knowing that every component came directly from his farm gave her a sense of pride and confidence in the product she was about to create.

The morning sun spilled through the window, casting a warm glow over her workspace. She felt as though her entire journey—from the quaint streets of Paris to the lush fields of Amish country—had led her to this very moment. With her notes laid out before her, Riley was prepared to tackle her first flavor: caramel vanilla. She wanted to recreate the magic of the ice cream she had tasted in Paris, a blend of rich, smoky caramel and fragrant vanilla, all balanced by the freshness of farm-sourced ingredients.

She started by pouring the fresh milk into a saucepan. The milk had a natural, earthy aroma that immediately filled the kitchen, grounding her in the reality of what she was creating. It wasn't just any milk; it was milk from cows raised on the pastures of Mr. Stoltzfus's farm, grazing on lush grasses and living naturally. She could feel the depth and quality in every drop, a testament to the dedication and care that had gone into its production.

Riley added a spoonful of raw honey to the milk, letting it melt into the mixture with a soft, golden glow. The honey had a floral, complex taste, a sweetness that felt connected to the earth itself. She had tasted many types of honey before, but this one was different—it had a unique character, a reminder of the flowers, the bees, and the gentle hands that had harvested it. As she stirred the milk and honey together, she couldn't help but think of the Parisian ice cream shop, where each ingredient carried a story, a journey from farm to spoon.

Next came the eggs, their yolks a brilliant yellow that reminded her of the sunrise over the fields in Amish country. She cracked them carefully, separating the yolks and whisking them into the mixture, the custard base taking on a beautiful golden hue. She knew that this step was crucial; French ice cream relied on a rich custard base, a balance of creaminess and depth that could only be achieved through careful preparation.

Once the custard was thickened to perfection, Riley added a generous swirl of caramel, its dark, smoky scent mingling with the creamy vanilla and floral honey. She could feel her senses come alive, the aroma filling the room and transporting her back to that first taste of *glace fermière* in Paris. It was as though the essence of her journey was distilled into this one moment, this one mixture that held all the flavors, all the memories she had gathered.

With the custard base prepared, she poured it into the ice cream maker, her hands steady but her heart racing with excitement. She watched as the machine began to churn, transforming the mixture into a smooth, thick, creamy delight. Each turn of the paddle felt like a step closer to realizing her dream, the ingredients from Mr. Stoltzfus's farm coming together in a dance of flavor and texture that she hoped would capture the hearts of her friends and family.

When the ice cream was finally ready, Riley scooped a small spoonful, bringing it to her lips with a mixture of excitement and trepidation. The flavor was deep and complex, the caramel dark and smoky, softened by the floral sweetness of the honey and balanced by the rich creaminess of the custard. It was everything she had hoped for, a blend of flavors that felt both familiar and new, a taste that echoed the magic of *glace fermière* while holding its own unique character.

Riley wanted to share this creation, to see if others would feel the same connection, the same joy that she had felt in Paris. She invited her parents and a few close friends over, eager to hear their feedback. Her kitchen quickly filled with laughter and chatter as everyone gathered around, eyeing the bowls of ice cream with a mixture of curiosity and anticipation.

Cynthia was the first to try it, her eyes lighting up as the flavors unfolded. "Riley, this is amazing," she said, her voice filled with pride. "I can taste each part—the caramel, the vanilla, even the honey. It's like nothing I've ever tasted."

Ron took a bite, nodding thoughtfully as he savored each spoonful. "This is the real deal," he said, his admiration evident. "I didn't know ice cream could taste like this. You've really created something special, Riley."

But her friends were a bit harder to impress. While some loved the unique flavors and creamy texture, others had suggestions for improvement. One friend mentioned that the ice cream was a bit too sweet, while another thought it could be creamier. Riley took their feedback seriously, jotting down notes and asking questions, determined to refine her recipe.

She realized that creating the perfect ice cream would take more than just a good recipe—it required patience, flexibility, and a willingness to listen. Each piece of criticism was a chance to improve, to bring her vision closer to the dream she held in her heart. She knew she had a long way to go, but she was willing to put in the work.

Over the next few weeks, Riley became a regular fixture in her kitchen, experimenting with flavors, adjusting ingredients, and consulting her notes from Amish country. She returned to Mr. Stoltzfus with questions, seeking his guidance on everything from dairy processing to honey harvesting. He was always patient, sharing his wisdom and reminding her of the importance of quality and care.

Through each conversation, Riley felt her connection to the farm deepen, her respect for the process and the people who worked the land growing with every visit. She wanted her ice cream to reflect the values Mr. Stoltzfus had taught her, to honor the dedication and love that went into each ingredient.

As her confidence grew, Riley began experimenting with new flavors, inspired by the organic ingredients Mr. Stoltzfus had provided. She created a honey lavender ice cream, using fresh honey and lavender flowers from his farm, the floral notes blending beautifully with the creamy base. She also developed a fig and almond flavor, a tribute to the flavors she had discovered in Paris, each bite a reminder of the journey that had brought her here.

She continued to host taste tests, inviting friends, family, and even a few neighbors to sample her creations. Each event was a learning experience, an opportunity to gather feedback and refine her recipes. She took each comment to heart, making adjustments and improvements, her ice cream evolving with each batch.

The process was challenging, filled with moments of doubt and frustration, but Riley never gave up. She knew that this was more than just ice cream—it was her dream, her connection to the land, her way of sharing the beauty she had found in both Paris and Amish country. She wanted each scoop to carry that essence, to tell the story of the ingredients, the farmers, and the journey that had brought her to this point.

With each taste test, Riley's dream became a little more real, a little closer to the vision she had carried in her heart since her first taste of *glace fermière*. She could see it in the smiles of her friends, the nods of approval from her parents, and the quiet pride in Mr. Stoltzfus's voice when he tasted her latest creations. She was no longer just a girl with a dream; she was a young entrepreneur, building something meaningful, something that connected her to her community and her values.

The day she brought her ice cream to a local diner marked a new milestone. Maria, the diner owner, listened intently as Riley shared her story, her vision for farm-to-table ice cream that honored the land and the people who cultivated it. Maria sampled each flavor, nodding in approval as she tasted the honey lavender, the caramel vanilla, and the fig almond. To Riley's delight, Maria agreed to feature her ice cream on the menu, giving her the first opportunity to reach a wider audience.

As Riley walked home that day, her heart was filled with a sense of accomplishment, a feeling that all the hard work, the late nights, and the early mornings had been worth it. She knew that there were many more challenges ahead, that her journey was just beginning. But for now, she allowed herself to savor the moment, to feel proud of what she had created.

Riley's ice cream was more than just a product; it was a connection to her past, her community, and her dreams. It was a testament to the power of dedication, of staying true to one's values, and of the simple beauty of farm-to-table ingredients. Each batch, each taste test, each smile from a satisfied customer brought her one step closer to her vision, a vision that she knew would continue to grow and evolve.

As she stood in her kitchen, surrounded by the tools of her craft, Riley felt a deep sense of gratitude. She knew that her journey was only beginning, that there were countless scoops of ice cream still to be made, each one a chance to share the magic she had discovered in Paris and Amish country. But for now, she was exactly where she was meant to be, a dreamer with a purpose, an artist with a mission, and a girl who had learned that sometimes, the sweetest dreams are the ones you create with your own hands.

Chapter 6: From Local to Lucrative

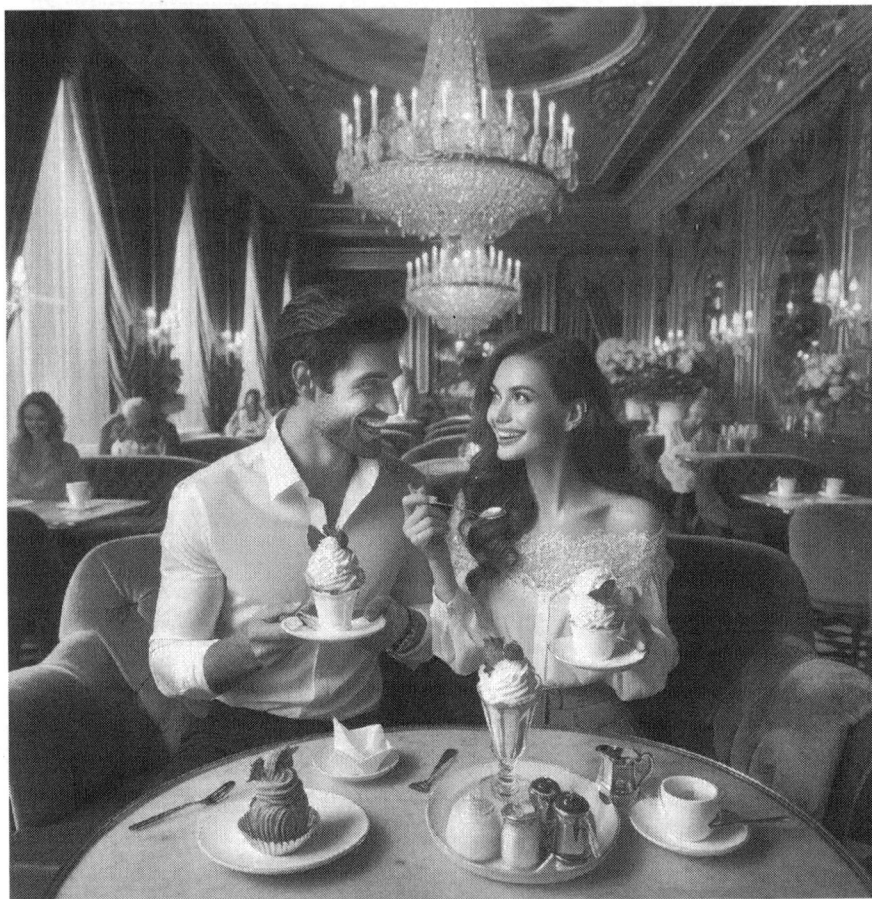

Riley's ice cream at Maria's diner quickly became the talk of the town. Locals who had visited out of curiosity soon became regular customers, each captivated by the creamy texture, deep flavors, and fresh ingredients of Riley's farm-to-table ice cream. Maria had creatively named the item "Farm Fresh Ice Cream by Riley," and the name alone sparked interest in the neighborhood. Riley's reputation began to spread through word of mouth, each bowl served a subtle endorsement that carried her dream further than she could have imagined.

As more people tasted Riley's ice cream, her story began to circulate in the community. Customers were enchanted by the idea of a young entrepreneur from Queens, committed to using only organic, farm-fresh ingredients sourced from Mr. Stoltzfus's Amish farm. Every scoop of ice cream seemed to capture the essence of her journey—from the Parisian inspiration to the pastoral landscapes of Pennsylvania. It was a whirlwind of new attention that Riley hadn't quite anticipated, but it was thrilling to watch her small venture flourish.

The response was more than just positive—it was fervent. Within weeks, Maria's diner began selling out of Riley's ice cream almost every day, customers arriving specifically to taste the unique, locally-sourced flavors. Riley was overjoyed, though she quickly realized that demand was beginning to exceed her small-scale production capabilities. She needed to adapt if she wanted to continue meeting the growing interest without compromising her product's quality.

One afternoon, Riley sat down with her parents in their cozy living room, a notebook balanced on her lap as she shared her ideas for expanding production. "A bakery down the street reached out to me," she explained, her eyes bright with excitement. "They want to partner with me and offer my ice cream as part of their dessert selection. They're even talking about using my caramel vanilla flavor for ice cream sandwiches!" Her parents listened intently, exchanging a proud glance as they saw how far their daughter's dream had come.

Cynthia was the first to voice the question on both their minds. "How do you think you'll keep up with all these orders?" she asked gently. Riley paused, her mind racing as she considered her options. She knew that her current setup—the family kitchen—was too limited for the level of production she now required. She needed a dedicated space, something that would allow her to expand her operation while still keeping everything fresh and authentic.

Ron suggested they consider converting their small garage into a production area, an idea that immediately sparked Riley's interest. The garage, currently filled with old tools, boxes, and other odds and ends, had plenty of potential. It was small but practical, a place that could be transformed into a mini production space if they could invest in the right equipment. "We'd need a bigger ice cream maker, a storage freezer, and maybe a few more shelves," she mused, her mind already racing with ideas for organizing the space.

With a plan beginning to take shape, Riley and her parents spent the next few days clearing out the garage, sorting through years of forgotten items to make room for her new business setup. The process was both nostalgic and invigorating, each box they moved a step closer to realizing Riley's vision. Once the space was cleared, Riley used her earnings from Maria's diner sales, along with a small loan from her parents, to purchase the equipment she needed. When the commercial-grade ice cream maker arrived, she felt a surge of pride. It was another sign that her dream was becoming tangible, her small business steadily growing.

As she set up her new workspace, Riley was meticulous, arranging each tool, each ingredient with care. She dedicated a section of the garage for the ingredients from Mr. Stoltzfus's farm, a constant reminder of the values that anchored her business. She filled jars with the raw honey, cream, fresh herbs, and fruits that he provided, each one a symbol of her commitment to authenticity and quality. Her workspace felt like an extension of herself, a place where her passion and purpose could flourish.

Once the setup was complete, Riley got to work refining her production process. She spent hours experimenting, testing methods for making larger batches without sacrificing the quality that her customers loved. She carefully timed each step, ensuring that every scoop maintained the texture and flavor that had set her ice cream apart. It was a meticulous process, each improvement a small but crucial step toward sustaining her dream.

With her expanded production capabilities, Riley's confidence grew. She began experimenting with seasonal flavors, inspired by the ingredients available from Mr. Stoltzfus's farm. Her first seasonal offering was a strawberry basil flavor in the spring, a fresh and vibrant blend that delighted her customers. In the fall, she introduced a pumpkin spice ice cream made with real pumpkin and warm spices, a cozy flavor that quickly became a hit. Each new flavor allowed Riley to express her creativity, to share a part of herself and the journey that had brought her here.

The community's response to her seasonal flavors was overwhelmingly positive. Customers appreciated the care and thought that went into each batch, the way Riley's ice cream celebrated both tradition and innovation. Her regulars became her biggest supporters, eagerly spreading the word to friends and family. The excitement around her business was infectious, and Riley found herself overwhelmed with gratitude for the community that had embraced her dream.

As demand continued to grow, Riley realized that she needed a way to manage her time more efficiently. Balancing her ice cream business with her schoolwork was becoming increasingly challenging, and she often found herself staying up late into the night to fill orders. She created a detailed schedule, mapping out her time to ensure that she could meet her obligations without burning out. It was a delicate balance, but she was determined to make it work.

Despite the challenges, each success fueled her determination to keep pushing forward. One day, a local food critic visited Maria's diner and ordered a bowl of Riley's caramel vanilla ice cream. Unbeknownst to her, this critic had a large following, his reviews known for their influence on local dining trends. Riley held her breath as she read his review the next day, her heart pounding as she scanned the page. To her relief and delight, the critic praised her ice cream, calling it "a triumph of simplicity and authenticity, a farm-to-table experience that elevates the humble scoop to an art form."

The review was a turning point. Riley's phone began ringing with inquiries from other local businesses interested in featuring her ice cream. She knew that her dream had reached a new level, that her ice cream had become something people sought out and talked about. It was exhilarating and humbling, a reminder of the journey she had undertaken and the hard work that had brought her this far.

But as her business grew, so did the demands on her time and energy. Riley began to feel the weight of her responsibilities, the pressure to meet the expectations of her customers while staying true to her values. She knew that expanding her business meant facing new challenges, each one a test of her resilience and commitment.

With the support of her parents, Riley continued to navigate the ups and downs of her growing business. She learned to trust her instincts, to make decisions that aligned with her vision even when it wasn't easy. She turned to her notebook often, a reminder of the dream that had started it all, the inspiration she had found in Paris, and the values she had learned from Mr. Stoltzfus.

Riley's success was a testament to her dedication and the support of her community. Each day brought new opportunities, new challenges, and new reasons to be grateful. She knew that her journey was far from over, that there were countless scoops of ice cream still to be made, each one a chance to share her story with the world.

Chapter 7: High School Hustle

Riley's alarm went off at 5 a.m., the shrill ring filling the quiet of her room. She groaned, pulling herself out of bed, her body heavy with the kind of exhaustion only a few hours of sleep could bring. But she didn't let herself linger; she had a routine to keep, one that she had crafted with care and dedication. By 5:15, she was downstairs in the garage, which had been transformed into her ice cream production space. She was surrounded by jars of ingredients, her ice cream maker humming softly as she prepared the first batch of the day.

The early hours were her time, a period when the world was quiet and she could focus solely on her work. As she measured ingredients and mixed flavors, she felt a sense of calm, a grounding that helped her balance the demands of her growing business with the pressures of high school. These mornings had become essential, a ritual that gave her the focus and energy she needed to make it through each day.

By the time her family started to wake up, Riley had already completed the first few tasks of the day. She would leave the ice cream to chill while she got ready for school, mentally organizing her tasks as she brushed her teeth and pulled her hair into a quick braid. Her parents admired her dedication, though they sometimes worried about the toll her business was taking on her. But Riley reassured them, promising she could handle it. She was determined to prove that she could balance her responsibilities, even if it meant making sacrifices.

When she arrived at John Bowne High School, she was greeted by the usual bustle of students, their voices filling the hallways as they chatted about weekend plans, social media trends, and schoolwork. Her friends had started to notice her intense routine, the way she seemed to juggle more responsibilities than the average teenager. They admired her ambition, though some of them teased her about her "double life" as an ice cream entrepreneur.

During lunch breaks, Riley often found herself retreating to the library, where she could focus on her work without distraction. Her notebook had become her constant companion, filled with sketches, ideas for new flavors, and lists of tasks she needed to complete. She used every spare moment to refine her business plans, to brainstorm strategies for reaching more customers and expanding her brand. It was exhausting, but it was also exhilarating—a reminder that she was building something meaningful, something that went beyond the walls of her high school.

Her teachers began to notice her dedication, the way she seemed focused and driven in a way that went beyond typical schoolwork. Some offered words of encouragement, praising her entrepreneurial spirit and her commitment to her dream. Others expressed concern, worried that she was taking on too much at such a young age. Riley appreciated their concern, but she was determined to prove that she could handle it. She balanced her responsibilities with care, refusing to let her grades suffer even as she poured more of herself into her business.

As the semester wore on, the demands of her business continued to grow. More restaurants had reached out, eager to feature her farm-to-table ice cream on their menus. Each new order brought a mixture of excitement and pressure, a reminder that her dream was becoming a reality but also a test of her ability to keep up. There were days when the workload felt overwhelming, when the demands of school and business seemed impossible to balance. But each time she felt like giving up, she reminded herself of the journey she had started, of the dream that had brought her this far.

Riley's parents remained her biggest supporters, always ready to lend a hand or offer a listening ear when the stress became too much. Cynthia helped with administrative tasks, managing orders and keeping track of inventory, while Ron took on the role of delivery driver, ensuring that each batch of ice cream reached its destination on time. Their support was invaluable, a reminder that Riley wasn't alone in her journey. They believed in her dream as much as she did, and their encouragement gave her the strength to keep going.

Despite the challenges, Riley's business continued to thrive. She found a rhythm, a routine that allowed her to keep up with both her schoolwork and her ice cream orders. It was a delicate balance, one that required discipline, resilience, and a willingness to adapt. But each success, each satisfied customer, reminded her of the journey she had started, the dream she was determined to see through.

One afternoon, Riley's guidance counselor called her into the office, curious about her unusual schedule and the buzz surrounding her business. "Riley, I've heard impressive things about your ice cream venture," she said, a warm smile on her face. "But I want to make sure you're not spreading yourself too thin. This is a lot for a high school student to handle."

Riley appreciated her counselor's concern, though she was determined to prove that she could manage both. She explained her passion for the business, her commitment to quality, and the dream that had driven her to start this journey. Her counselor listened thoughtfully, nodding as Riley shared her vision and the values that anchored her work.

"You have a lot of ambition, Riley," she said gently. "But remember to take care of yourself. This is a marathon, not a sprint." Riley took her words to heart, recognizing the importance of balance and self-care. She began to set boundaries, carving out time for herself and her family, moments of rest that gave her the strength to keep going.

Through it all, Riley's grades remained steady, a testament to her discipline and focus. She knew that her education was important, that it provided a foundation for her future success. She approached her studies with the same determination she brought to her business, refusing to let her grades suffer.

Riley's guidance counselor's advice stayed with her, a reminder to take things one step at a time. She began implementing small changes, moments of rest and self-care that helped her find balance amidst the chaos. Instead of working late into the night, she set a strict bedtime, making sure she got enough sleep to keep up with her demanding schedule. She also started using weekends as a time to recharge, spending time with friends and family, activities that filled her with energy and motivation.

One Saturday, Riley joined her friends for a picnic in the park, something she hadn't done in months. As they laughed and shared stories, she realized how much she had missed these simple moments, the joy of being a teenager. Her friends were supportive, though they often joked about her "ice cream empire." They didn't fully understand her responsibilities, but they cheered her on, excited to see her business grow.

The outing reminded Riley of the importance of balance, of finding joy in the journey rather than being consumed by the destination. She returned home that evening feeling refreshed, her mind clearer and more focused. She approached her work with renewed energy, each scoop of ice cream a reminder of the dream that had brought her here. She knew that finding balance was a continuous process, one that required intention and self-awareness.

As her business continued to grow, Riley began receiving invitations to local events, markets, and fairs, each one an opportunity to showcase her ice cream. These events were both thrilling and nerve-wracking;

she was excited to reach new customers but anxious about representing her brand in a public setting. She spent hours preparing, perfecting her setup, and practicing her pitch, determined to make a lasting impression.

At her first farmers' market, Riley set up a small stall, her ice cream displayed in colorful tubs with handmade labels. She had chosen a few of her most popular flavors, including caramel vanilla, honey lavender, and strawberry basil, each one a reflection of her commitment to farm-to-table ingredients. As customers approached her stall, Riley greeted them with a smile, sharing the story behind her ice cream and the values that had guided her journey.

The response was overwhelming. People were intrigued by the idea of a young entrepreneur with a dedication to quality and sustainability. They sampled her ice cream, nodding in approval as they savored the rich, creamy flavors. Riley's heart swelled with pride as she watched their reactions, each satisfied customer a reminder of the impact her dream was making.

The success of the farmers' market encouraged Riley to pursue more public events, each one an opportunity to reach a wider audience and build her brand. She developed a routine, a checklist of tasks to ensure that each event ran smoothly. She refined her setup, adding small touches like hand-painted signs and a chalkboard menu that displayed her seasonal flavors. Her stall became a familiar sight at local events, customers eagerly lining up to taste her latest creations.

But with each new success came new challenges. Riley found herself juggling multiple responsibilities, each one demanding her time and attention. She learned to prioritize, focusing on the tasks that mattered most and letting go of the things that didn't. It was a lesson in resilience, a reminder that success required both determination and adaptability.

Her parents continued to support her, always ready to lend a hand or offer a word of encouragement. Cynthia helped with event logistics, managing orders and inventory, while Ron handled deliveries and setup. Their unwavering support reminded Riley that she wasn't alone in her journey, that her success was a shared achievement, built on the foundation of family and community.

As the school year progressed, Riley's schedule became increasingly demanding. She often found herself studying for exams in the early hours of the morning, her notebook filled with both business plans and study notes. Her teachers noticed her dedication, impressed by her ability to balance her academic and entrepreneurial pursuits. Some offered additional support, providing extra resources or tutoring sessions to help her keep up with her studies.

Despite the challenges, Riley's grades remained steady, a testament to her discipline and focus. She approached her schoolwork with the same determination she brought to her business, refusing to let one priority overshadow the other. It was a balancing act, a continuous effort to keep both her dreams and her responsibilities in harmony.

One day, as Riley walked through the halls of her high school, she overheard a group of students talking about her ice cream business. They mentioned her stall at the farmers' market, praising the flavors and the quality of her products. Riley's heart swelled with pride; it was a surreal moment, a reminder that her dream was resonating with people beyond her immediate circle. She felt a renewed sense of purpose, a motivation to continue building her business and sharing her story with the world.

Her friends, too, began to take notice, supporting her venture in ways they hadn't before. They would occasionally stop by her stall at events, cheering her on and spreading the word about her business. Their support meant the world to Riley, a reminder that her dream was not just her own but a shared journey, one that connected her to the people who believed in her.

But as her business grew, so did the pressures and responsibilities. Riley found herself facing moments of doubt, times when the workload felt overwhelming and the future uncertain. There were nights when she questioned her abilities, wondering if she was truly capable of balancing everything. But each time, she reminded herself of the journey she had started, the passion that had fueled her dream, and the support of her family and friends.

One evening, after a particularly challenging day, Riley sat down with her parents, her voice filled with frustration and fatigue. She shared her doubts, her fears about the future, and the pressures she felt to succeed. Cynthia and Ron listened patiently, offering words of encouragement and reminding her of the strength and resilience she had shown throughout her journey.

"You've already accomplished so much, Riley," Cynthia said, her voice gentle but firm. "Remember, it's okay to take a step back and breathe. You're allowed to pace yourself."

Riley nodded, her heart filled with gratitude for her parents' unwavering support. Their words reminded her of the importance of self-compassion, of allowing herself the space to grow without expecting perfection. She took a deep breath, feeling a renewed sense of clarity and purpose. She knew that her journey was far from over, but she was ready to face each challenge with resilience and determination.

With a new sense of balance, Riley continued to pursue her dreams, each day a step closer to the vision she held in her heart. She knew that the road ahead would be filled with obstacles, but she was confident in her ability to overcome them. She was no longer just a high school student with a dream; she was a young entrepreneur, a creator, a girl who had learned to balance her passions with her responsibilities.

As she stood in her garage, surrounded by the tools of her trade, Riley felt a deep sense of gratitude. She was building something meaningful, something that connected her to her community, her family, and her own sense of purpose. Each scoop of ice cream was a testament to her journey, a reminder of the dream that had brought her this far. She was ready to face whatever challenges lay ahead, confident in her vision and her ability to make it a reality.

Riley's guidance counselor's advice stayed with her, a reminder to take things one step at a time. She began implementing small changes, moments of rest and self-care that helped her find balance amidst the chaos. Instead of working late into the night, she set a strict bedtime, making sure she got enough sleep to keep up with her demanding schedule. She also started using weekends as a time to recharge, spending time with friends and family, activities that filled her with energy and motivation.

One Saturday, Riley joined her friends for a picnic in the park, something she hadn't done in months. As they laughed and shared stories, she realized how much she had missed these simple moments, the joy of being a teenager. Her friends were supportive, though they often joked about her "ice cream empire." They didn't fully understand her responsibilities, but they cheered her on, excited to see her business grow.

The outing reminded Riley of the importance of balance, of finding joy in the journey rather than being consumed by the destination. She returned home that evening feeling refreshed, her mind clearer and more focused. She approached her work with renewed energy, each scoop of ice cream a reminder of the dream that had brought her here. She knew that finding balance was a continuous process, one that required intention and self-awareness.

As her business continued to grow, Riley began receiving invitations to local events, markets, and fairs, each one an opportunity to showcase her ice cream. These events were both thrilling and nerve-wracking; she was excited to reach new customers but anxious about representing her brand in a public setting. She spent hours preparing, perfecting her setup, and practicing her pitch, determined to make a lasting impression.

At her first farmers' market, Riley set up a small stall, her ice cream displayed in colorful tubs with handmade labels. She had chosen a few of her most popular flavors, including caramel vanilla, honey lavender, and strawberry basil, each one a reflection of her commitment to farm-to-table ingredients. As customers approached her stall, Riley greeted them with a smile, sharing the story behind her ice cream and the values that had guided her journey.

The response was overwhelming. People were intrigued by the idea of a young entrepreneur with a dedication to quality and sustainability. They sampled her ice cream, nodding in approval as they savored the rich, creamy flavors. Riley's heart swelled with pride as she watched their reactions, each satisfied customer a reminder of the impact her dream was making.

The success of the farmers' market encouraged Riley to pursue more public events, each one an opportunity to reach a wider audience and build her brand. She developed a routine, a checklist of tasks to ensure that each event ran smoothly. She refined her setup, adding small touches like hand-painted signs and a chalkboard menu that displayed her seasonal flavors. Her stall became a familiar sight at local events, customers eagerly lining up to taste her latest creations.

But with each new success came new challenges. Riley found herself juggling multiple responsibilities, each one demanding her time and attention. She learned to prioritize, focusing on the tasks that mattered most and letting go of the things that didn't. It was a lesson in resilience, a reminder that success required both determination and adaptability.

Her parents continued to support her, always ready to lend a hand or offer a word of encouragement. Cynthia helped with event logistics, managing orders and inventory, while Ron handled deliveries and setup. Their unwavering support reminded Riley that she wasn't alone in her journey, that her success was a shared achievement, built on the foundation of family and community.

As the school year progressed, Riley's schedule became increasingly demanding. She often found herself studying for exams in the early hours of the morning, her notebook filled with both business plans and study notes. Her teachers noticed her dedication, impressed by her ability to balance her academic and entrepreneurial pursuits. Some offered additional support, providing extra resources or tutoring sessions to help her keep up with her studies.

Despite the challenges, Riley's grades remained steady, a testament to her discipline and focus. She approached her schoolwork with the same determination she brought to her business, refusing to let one priority overshadow the other. It was a balancing act, a continuous effort to keep both her dreams and her responsibilities in harmony.

One day, as Riley walked through the halls of her high school, she overheard a group of students talking about her ice cream business. They mentioned her stall at the farmers' market, praising the flavors and the quality of her products. Riley's heart swelled with pride; it was a surreal moment, a reminder that her dream was resonating with people beyond her immediate circle. She felt a renewed sense of purpose, a motivation to continue building her business and sharing her story with the world.

Her friends, too, began to take notice, supporting her venture in ways they hadn't before. They would occasionally stop by her stall at events, cheering her on and spreading the word about her business. Their support meant the world to Riley, a reminder that her dream was not just her own but a shared journey, one that connected her to the people who believed in her.

But as her business grew, so did the pressures and responsibilities. Riley found herself facing moments of doubt, times when the workload felt overwhelming and the future uncertain. There were nights when she questioned her abilities, wondering if she was truly capable of balancing everything. But each time, she reminded herself of the journey she had started, the passion that had fueled her dream, and the support of her family and friends.

One evening, after a particularly challenging day, Riley sat down with her parents, her voice filled with frustration and fatigue. She shared her doubts, her fears about the future, and the pressures she felt to succeed. Cynthia and Ron listened patiently, offering words of encouragement and reminding her of the strength and resilience she had shown throughout her journey.

"You've already accomplished so much, Riley," Cynthia said, her voice gentle but firm. "Remember, it's okay to take a step back and breathe. You're allowed to pace yourself."

Riley nodded, her heart filled with gratitude for her parents' unwavering support. Their words reminded her of the importance of self-compassion, of allowing herself the space to grow without expecting perfection. She took a deep breath, feeling a renewed sense of clarity and purpose. She knew that her journey was far from over, but she was ready to face each challenge with resilience and determination.

With a new sense of balance, Riley continued to pursue her dreams, each day a step closer to the vision she held in her heart. She knew that the road ahead would be filled with obstacles, but she was confident in her ability to overcome them. She was no longer just a high school student with a dream; she was a young entrepreneur, a creator, a girl who had learned to balance her passions with her responsibilities.

As she stood in her garage, surrounded by the tools of her trade, Riley felt a deep sense of gratitude. She was building something meaningful, something that connected her to her community, her family, and her own sense of purpose. Each scoop of ice cream was a testament to her journey, a reminder of the dream that had brought her this far. She was ready to face whatever challenges lay ahead, confident in her vision and her ability to make it a reality.

Chapter 8: Marketing Magic

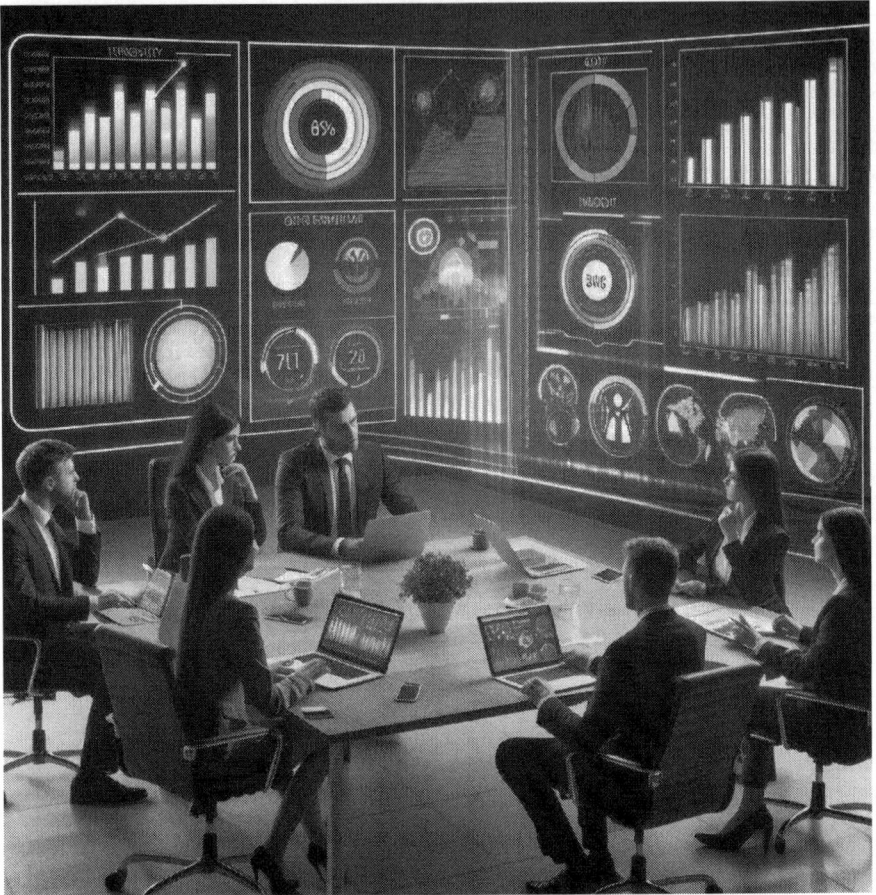

Riley sat at her desk, her sketchbook open and a pencil in hand. She'd spent the past few days brainstorming ideas for her ice cream brand, pages filled with doodles, logo concepts, and notes on colors and themes. She wanted her brand to tell a story, to capture the essence of the farm-to-table philosophy that defined her ice cream. As she flipped through her sketches, Riley felt a surge of excitement. This was her chance to give her business an identity, a look and feel that would resonate with her customers and make her product stand out.

She started with the basics, thinking about the elements that mattered most to her. Her ice cream was more than just a product—it was a tribute to her journey, from the inspiration she found in Paris to the partnership she had formed with Mr. Stoltzfus's farm. She wanted her branding to reflect the natural, wholesome ingredients she used, the dedication to quality, and the connection to the land. Her mind filled with images of rolling fields, rustic barns, and jars of fresh ingredients, each one a piece of the story she wanted to tell.

Riley knew that her brand needed a name that captured this essence. She toyed with different ideas, writing them down and saying them aloud to see how they sounded. She considered names like "Pure Creamery" and "Farm to Cone," each one hinting at her commitment to freshness and sustainability. But none of them felt quite right. She wanted something that was uniquely hers, something that would make people think of quality and care.

After hours of brainstorming, Riley finally landed on a name that felt perfect: "Harvest Creamery." The word "Harvest" spoke to the natural, seasonal ingredients she sourced from Mr. Stoltzfus's farm, while "Creamery" conveyed the artisan, small-batch quality that set her ice cream apart. She said it aloud a few times, savoring the sound. It felt right, a name that held both simplicity and depth, a name that would grow with her business.

With her brand name settled, Riley moved on to the logo. She wanted something simple but memorable, a design that reflected the farm-to-table essence of her product. She sketched different ideas, playing with shapes and colors. She drew a small barn with rolling hills behind it, a cow grazing in a pasture, and a scoop of ice cream surrounded by leaves. Each sketch felt closer to what she wanted, each one capturing a piece of the story she wanted to tell.

After a few drafts, Riley landed on a design that made her heart skip a beat. It was a simple circle, with the words "Harvest Creamery" in a rustic, handwritten font. Inside the circle, she had drawn a small barn with fields stretching out behind it, a nod to Mr. Stoltzfus's farm. The design was clean, charming, and authentic, a perfect reflection of her brand. She felt a surge of pride as she looked at the logo. It was her vision brought to life, a symbol of everything her business stood for.

Next, Riley turned her attention to packaging. She wanted her ice cream containers to be as eco-friendly as possible, a commitment to sustainability that aligned with her values. She researched different options, from biodegradable paper cups to compostable lids, each one a step toward reducing her environmental impact. She wanted her customers to feel good about their choice, to know that every scoop of ice cream they enjoyed was part of a larger commitment to the planet.

She chose a soft, earthy color palette for her packaging, with shades of cream, green, and brown that evoked the natural ingredients she used. The containers would feature her logo on the front, with a small label that listed the flavor and a short description of the ingredients. She kept the design simple, letting the quality of the product speak for itself. Each container felt like a small piece of art, a blend of form and function that represented her brand's values.

As she finalized the packaging, Riley couldn't help but feel a sense of accomplishment. She had created a brand that was more than just a logo and a name—it was a reflection of her journey, her commitment to quality, and her passion for farm-to-table ingredients. It was everything she had dreamed of, a brand that would resonate with her customers and make her product stand out.

With her branding complete, Riley turned her attention to marketing. She knew that social media would be a powerful tool for reaching new customers and building a loyal following. Instagram seemed like the perfect platform, a place where she could showcase the beauty of her ice cream and share the story behind each flavor. She created an account for Harvest Creamery, carefully curating each post to reflect the natural, wholesome essence of her brand.

Her first post was a photo of her caramel vanilla ice cream, set against a rustic wooden backdrop with fresh vanilla beans and a jar of caramel beside it. The caption read: "Introducing Harvest Creamery's Caramel Vanilla—made with farm-fresh dairy, raw honey, and a touch of smoky caramel. Taste the difference of farm-to-table ingredients!" She hit "post" and watched as the likes and comments began to roll in, each one a small step toward building her audience.

As her Instagram following grew, Riley started experimenting with different types of content. She posted photos of her ingredients, snapshots of her setup in the garage, and behind-the-scenes glimpses of her production process. She wanted her followers to feel connected to the journey, to see the care and dedication that went into each batch of ice cream. Each post was a piece of the story, a window into the world of Harvest Creamery.

Riley also reached out to local food bloggers, inviting them to try her ice cream and share their experiences with their followers. She sent them small packages with a handwritten note, explaining her commitment to quality and her journey from Queens to Amish country. The bloggers were intrigued, eager to support a young entrepreneur with a passion for sustainability and farm-to-table ingredients.

The response was overwhelmingly positive. The bloggers praised the quality of her ice cream, describing the flavors as "rich, creamy, and full of natural goodness." They shared photos and stories about Harvest Creamery, tagging Riley's account and encouraging their followers to give it a try. Riley watched as her follower count grew, each new like and comment a testament to the impact her story was making.

With her growing fan base, Riley decided to expand her marketing efforts. She created a series of posts that highlighted each flavor, sharing the story behind the ingredients and the inspiration behind the taste. She posted about her strawberry basil ice cream, explaining how the fresh strawberries and hint of basil created a unique, refreshing flavor. She shared the story of her honey lavender ice cream, a blend of floral honey and delicate lavender that evoked the beauty of spring.

Each post was carefully crafted, a blend of storytelling and photography that captured the essence of Harvest Creamery. Riley found that her followers were drawn to the authenticity of her brand, the way each flavor told a story and connected them to the land. She received messages from customers who had tried her ice cream at local events, each one filled with words of encouragement and praise.

As her online presence grew, so did the demand for her ice cream. More local restaurants and cafes reached out, eager to feature her product on their menus. Riley was thrilled, though she knew that keeping up with the demand would be a challenge. She worked tirelessly, balancing her social media efforts with her production schedule, each day a new opportunity to reach more people and share her vision.

The success of her branding and social media efforts was a turning point for Riley. She had created a brand that resonated with people, a brand that stood for quality, sustainability, and a connection to the land. She knew that her journey was far from over, but she was confident in her vision and her ability to make it a reality.

As Harvest Creamery continued to grow, Riley remained dedicated to her values, always striving to create a product that reflected her passion for farm-to-table ingredients. She knew that her brand was more than just a name or a logo—it was a story, a journey, and a testament to the power of following one's dreams.

Each day brought new challenges and new opportunities, each one a step closer to her vision. Riley was ready to face whatever lay ahead, confident in the brand she had built and the support of the community that had embraced her dream. She was no longer just a high school student with a passion for ice cream; she was a young entrepreneur, a creator, and a storyteller, sharing her journey one scoop at a time.

Chapter 9: Business is Booming

Riley sat back in her chair, surrounded by stacks of order sheets and emails from restaurants, cafes, and eateries from all around New York and New Jersey. Each request felt surreal—a growing list of businesses excited to feature her farm-to-table ice cream on their menus. She read through each message, her heart racing with both excitement and a hint of overwhelm. Harvest Creamery had become more successful than she had ever imagined, and as the demand grew, so did the pressure to meet it.

Everywhere she looked, Riley saw evidence of the dream she had built from scratch. She had started out small, producing ice cream in her family's garage, but now her brand had become something bigger, something that resonated with people. She knew, however, that this level of success came with new responsibilities and challenges. Keeping up with orders on her own was no longer an option. She needed help.

Her thoughts immediately turned to Mr. Stoltzfus, the farmer who had been with her from the beginning. His dedication to quality and sustainability had been instrumental in building her brand, and she knew that if anyone could help her meet this demand, it was him. She reached out to him that evening, explaining the overwhelming number of orders she was receiving and her need to scale up production without compromising the integrity of her product.

Mr. Stoltzfus listened carefully, nodding as he absorbed the details. When Riley finished, he smiled warmly. "You know, Riley, I've seen this coming for a while," he said. "You've got something special here, and it's clear that people are drawn to the quality and values you stand for. I think it's time we bring in some extra hands."

Riley's eyes lit up with relief and gratitude. "Do you think the community would be willing to help?" she asked, knowing the Amish were often hesitant about expanding beyond their local markets. But she also knew that they valued hard work, quality, and supporting one another. If anyone could understand her mission, it was them.

"I'll reach out to our cooperative," Mr. Stoltzfus replied. "We have a network of farmers and workers who believe in the same values as you do. If they're willing, we can set up a production line here on the farm and distribute the workload. I think they'll be excited to take part in something like this."

The next few days were a whirlwind of planning and coordination. Mr. Stoltzfus held meetings with farmers from the cooperative, explaining Riley's business model and her commitment to quality. The response was overwhelmingly positive. The community was eager to help, thrilled at the idea of their ingredients reaching customers all over New York and New Jersey. Together, they began setting up a production space on Mr. Stoltzfus's farm, complete with stations for dairy processing, mixing, and packaging.

The expansion required careful planning and dedication, but the Amish community was skilled at working together, each member contributing their talents to the operation. Farmers who had expertise in dairy production handled the milk and cream, ensuring that each batch was as fresh and pure as possible. Others, who specialized in harvesting, provided the fruits and herbs that gave Riley's ice cream its unique flavors. It was a collaborative effort, each person bringing their skills and dedication to the table.

Riley felt a deep sense of gratitude as she watched the cooperative come together. She visited the farm regularly, observing the process and providing guidance where needed. She worked closely with Mr. Stoltzfus, discussing each detail of production, from the timing of milk delivery to the exact temperatures required for churning. She wanted to make sure that every scoop of ice cream retained the quality her customers had come to expect, even as they scaled up to meet demand.

The cooperative's setup allowed Riley to focus on other aspects of her business, but she quickly realized that managing the logistics of her growing enterprise required additional support. She needed a team to handle marketing, distribution, and order management, people who could help her keep everything running smoothly. She turned to her father, Ron, for advice, knowing that he had experience with logistics and business management.

Ron was eager to help, excited to see how far Riley's dream had come. Together, they started looking for a small office space where they could set up a headquarters for Harvest Creamery. After a few weeks of searching, they found the perfect spot in Bayside, Queens. The office was small but functional, with enough room for a few desks, a meeting area, and storage for supplies. It was a space where Riley could manage her business, meet with clients, and coordinate with her new team.

The process of hiring her first employees was both exciting and nerve-wracking. Riley wanted people who believed in her vision, who understood the importance of quality and sustainability. She held interviews, carefully selecting individuals who shared her values and had the skills needed to support her business. She hired a marketing manager to handle social media and outreach, a distribution coordinator to oversee deliveries, and an administrative assistant to manage orders and customer inquiries.

With her team in place, Riley felt a new sense of stability and organization. Each person brought their unique strengths to the business, helping her expand her reach and improve her efficiency. The marketing manager took over her Instagram account, creating beautiful, engaging posts that showcased the story behind each flavor. The distribution coordinator worked closely with local trucking companies, setting up a reliable delivery network that ensured her ice cream reached its destination on time and in perfect condition.

The administrative assistant managed the growing influx of orders, answering customer questions and keeping track of each request. It was a relief for Riley to have support, to know that she could focus on the bigger picture while her team handled the day-to-day tasks. She felt a renewed sense of energy and purpose, her dream expanding in ways she had never imagined.

The new office in Bayside quickly became a hub of activity. Riley and her team spent hours each day coordinating orders, managing inventory, and brainstorming new marketing strategies. The walls were lined with posters of her flavors, each one a reminder of the journey that had brought her here. The office was small, but it was filled with energy and excitement, a place where ideas flowed freely and everyone worked together toward a common goal.

As demand continued to grow, Riley found herself fielding requests from larger restaurants and even small grocery stores. The idea of selling her ice cream in retail locations was thrilling, though it presented new challenges. She needed to ensure that her product could withstand the longer shelf life required for retail, while still retaining its farm-to-table freshness and quality. She consulted with her team, exploring options for packaging and storage that would maintain the integrity of her ice cream.

Mr. Stoltzfus and the cooperative were invaluable partners in this effort. They worked with Riley to adjust the production process, experimenting with different methods to ensure that the ice cream stayed fresh and flavorful for retail distribution. The Amish community took pride in their work, each person committed to upholding the values that defined Harvest Creamery. Their dedication was evident in every batch, a testament to the power of collaboration and shared vision.

With the new packaging in place, Riley began reaching out to local grocery stores, offering samples and sharing the story behind her brand. She met with store managers, explaining her commitment to sustainability and her partnership with the Amish community. Many were impressed by her dedication and the quality of her product, eager to support a young entrepreneur with a passion for farm-to-table ingredients.

Soon, Harvest Creamery ice cream began appearing on the shelves of small, independent grocery stores across New York and New Jersey. The sight of her product in a retail setting was surreal, a tangible representation of the dream she had nurtured since her trip to Paris. She felt a deep sense of pride and accomplishment, knowing that her hard work and determination had brought her to this point.

The response from customers was overwhelmingly positive. People were drawn to the authenticity of her brand, the way each flavor told a story and connected them to the land. Riley received messages from customers who had tried her ice cream for the first time, each one filled with words of encouragement and praise. Her brand was resonating with people, a reminder of the power of following one's dreams and staying true to one's values.

As the business continued to expand, Riley faced new challenges and responsibilities. She was now managing a team, coordinating with the cooperative, and overseeing distribution across multiple locations. It was a demanding role, one that required resilience, adaptability, and a willingness to learn. But Riley embraced each challenge with enthusiasm, grateful for the opportunity to grow and evolve as an entrepreneur.

Her relationship with her team grew stronger as they worked together to navigate the demands of a booming business. They celebrated each success, from new partnerships with restaurants to glowing reviews from customers. The office in Bayside became a close-knit community, a place where everyone was invested in the success of Harvest Creamery. Riley felt a sense of camaraderie and support, a reminder that her journey was no longer just her own.

Through it all, her parents remained her biggest supporters, always ready to lend a hand or offer a listening ear. Ron continued to play a vital role in the business, handling logistics and helping with deliveries. Cynthia provided emotional support, reminding Riley of the importance of balance and self-care. Their love and encouragement were a constant source of strength, a reminder that she was never alone in her journey.

Riley's journey from a young girl with a dream to a successful business owner was a testament to the power of resilience, passion, and community. She knew that the road ahead would be filled with new challenges, but she was ready to face each one with confidence and determination. Her brand had become more than just a business—it was a story, a legacy, and a reminder that dreams were worth pursuing.

Each day brought new opportunities and new reasons to be grateful. Riley was no longer just a high school student with a passion for ice cream; she was a young entrepreneur, a creator, and a leader. She had built something meaningful, something that connected her to her community, her family, and her own sense of purpose.

As she looked out over the bustling office, surrounded by her team and the fruits of her labor, Riley felt a deep sense of fulfillment. She was building something that mattered, something that would inspire others to follow their dreams. And with each scoop of ice cream, each new customer, and each new partnership, she was reminded of the journey that had brought her here, and the limitless possibilities that lay ahead.

Chapter 10: Competing with the Big Brands

The email arrived in the middle of a busy Monday morning. Riley was in the midst of her routine, reviewing orders and going over distribution schedules with her team when a new message popped up on her screen. She clicked on it, her curiosity piqued, only to find a message from a national food distribution company expressing interest in her ice cream. They wanted to discuss potential partnerships and explore the possibility of carrying her product in larger grocery chains across the East Coast.

Riley's heart skipped a beat. The thought of her farm-to-table ice cream sitting alongside major brands in big-name grocery stores was both thrilling and intimidating. It was the kind of opportunity she had dreamed of, a chance to take her brand to the next level. But as she read further into the email, doubts began to creep in. She knew that stepping into a larger market meant competing with established brands, companies that had resources, reach, and influence that far exceeded her own. She wasn't sure if Harvest Creamery was ready for that level of competition.

Her team was just as excited as she was, urging her to take the meeting and explore the possibilities. "This could be huge for us, Riley," her marketing manager said, her eyes alight with excitement. "Imagine Harvest Creamery on the shelves of major stores all over the region. It's the kind of exposure that could change everything."

Riley nodded, feeling the weight of their enthusiasm and expectations. She agreed to the meeting, knowing that she couldn't pass up the opportunity without at least hearing what they had to offer. She spent the next few days preparing, researching the company and the logistics of entering a larger market. She knew that this wasn't just about expanding her reach; it was about finding a way to compete with the big brands while staying true to her values.

The meeting took place in a sleek office building downtown, the kind of place where polished executives in tailored suits discussed numbers and strategies with effortless confidence. Riley felt out of place, a young entrepreneur surrounded by seasoned professionals, but she reminded herself of the journey that had brought her here. She had built something special, something that resonated with people, and she was determined to protect that, no matter what.

The representatives from the distribution company were friendly and enthusiastic, eager to explore the potential of working with Harvest Creamery. They praised her brand, her commitment to quality, and the story behind her farm-to-table approach. But as the conversation progressed, Riley began to see the challenges that lay ahead. The company wanted her to adjust her production process to meet their requirements, suggesting changes that would increase efficiency but compromise the freshness and authenticity of her ingredients.

Riley listened carefully, her heart sinking as they outlined their expectations. They wanted her to use cheaper ingredients, to streamline her process in a way that would cut costs but sacrifice the quality that defined her brand. They assured her that these changes were necessary to compete with larger brands, to survive in a market dominated by big names and high-volume production. But Riley knew that these adjustments would undermine everything Harvest Creamery stood for.

After the meeting, she felt a mix of disappointment and frustration. She had hoped for a partnership that would allow her to expand while staying true to her values, but it was clear that entering the mainstream market would require compromises she wasn't willing to make. She returned to her office in Bayside, her mind racing as she considered her options. She knew that Harvest Creamery's unique selling point was its authenticity, its connection to the land and the community. Without that, her brand would be just another name on a shelf.

As the days passed, Riley's dilemma grew more pressing. She began receiving inquiries from other companies, each one expressing interest in her product but with similar demands for changes in production. The pressure to compete was mounting, and she could feel herself being pulled in multiple directions, each one a step away from the values that had guided her from the beginning. She knew that expanding her brand was essential to its survival, but she was determined to do it on her own terms.

In the midst of this struggle, Riley faced a new set of challenges: legal hurdles and industry regulations that she hadn't anticipated. Larger companies were protective of their market share, and as her brand gained popularity, she began receiving notices from corporate lawyers warning her about potential trademark issues and compliance with industry standards. She was baffled at first, unsure of how to navigate the complex world of food regulations and intellectual property rights.

Feeling overwhelmed, Riley sought advice from a local business attorney, someone who could help her understand the legal landscape and protect her brand. The attorney explained that as Harvest Creamery grew, she would need to take steps to protect her intellectual property, to ensure that her brand name, logo, and recipes were secure.

Riley listened carefully, taking notes as she learned about trademarks, patents, and compliance with industry regulations.

The attorney also warned her about the tactics used by larger companies to suppress competition, explaining that many big brands filed lawsuits and issued warnings to smaller competitors as a way to intimidate them. Riley felt a surge of frustration as she realized the extent of the challenges she faced. She had worked tirelessly to build her brand, to create something meaningful, and now she was being forced to navigate a world that seemed designed to protect the interests of large corporations.

But Riley was determined to protect her dream. She filed for a trademark on the Harvest Creamery name, ensuring that her brand would be legally protected. She worked closely with the attorney to review her production process, making adjustments to ensure compliance with industry standards while maintaining the quality and authenticity of her ice cream. It was a learning curve, a crash course in the complexities of the food industry, but Riley was willing to put in the work.

Despite the obstacles, Riley found strength in her commitment to her mission. She knew that Harvest Creamery's success was built on its unique identity, its connection to the community, and its dedication to quality. She realized that competing with big brands didn't mean trying to imitate them; it meant standing out, focusing on the things that made her product special. She began to shift her perspective, seeing the competition not as a threat but as an opportunity to differentiate herself.

With this renewed sense of purpose, Riley turned her attention to her marketing strategy. She wanted to highlight the values that set Harvest Creamery apart, to show customers that her ice cream was more than just a product—it was a story, a journey, and a commitment to sustainability. She worked closely with her marketing team, brainstorming ideas for campaigns that would emphasize the farm-to-table philosophy and the partnerships with local farmers that defined her brand.

Her team suggested a series of short videos for social media, each one featuring a different aspect of her production process. They filmed Mr. Stoltzfus and the Amish cooperative, showing the care and dedication that went into every batch of ice cream. They captured the beauty of the fields, the freshness of the ingredients, and the smiles of the farmers who made it all possible. Each video was a glimpse into the world of Harvest Creamery, a reminder of the values that set it apart from the competition.

The response was overwhelmingly positive. Customers loved the transparency, the authenticity, and the sense of connection that came with each scoop of ice cream. Riley received messages from people who had seen the videos, each one filled with words of encouragement and appreciation for her commitment to quality. Her following grew, and more restaurants reached out, eager to support a brand that stood for something real and meaningful.

As Harvest Creamery's popularity continued to grow, Riley felt a renewed sense of confidence. She knew that the competition from big brands would always be there, but she was no longer intimidated. She had found a way to navigate the challenges, to protect her brand, and to stay true to her mission. She realized that her strength lay in her authenticity, in the community connections that made her brand unique.

Each day brought new challenges, but Riley was ready to face them with resilience and determination. She knew that the road ahead would be filled with obstacles, but she was confident in her vision and her ability to make it a reality. Harvest Creamery was more than just a business—it was a legacy, a reminder that dreams were worth pursuing, no matter the challenges.

As she looked out over her office window, surrounded by her team and the fruits of her labor, Riley felt a deep sense of fulfillment. She had built something meaningful, something that connected her to her community, her family, and her own sense of purpose. Each scoop of ice cream was a testament to her journey, a reminder of the dream that had brought her this far. And with each new customer, each new partnership, she was reminded of the limitless possibilities that lay ahead.

Chapter 11: Riley Graduates from High School and Wins a Scholarship

Riley's last semester in high school had finally arrived, and she could hardly believe it. The hallways of John Bowne High School, so familiar after four years, held a bittersweet feeling for her now. These halls had seen her grow in ways she had never imagined—from a quiet freshman with a dream to an accomplished young entrepreneur managing a full-fledged business, Harvest Creamery. And now, after countless early mornings and late nights, graduation was just around the corner.

Every day felt like a delicate balancing act as Riley split her time between final exams, group projects, and keeping her business running smoothly. She was constantly on the go, but the thrill of her accomplishments made the chaos worthwhile. Harvest Creamery was thriving, with new orders coming in from cafes and restaurants across New York and New Jersey, and she managed her expanding team with as much focus as she dedicated to her studies. Her teachers were quick to notice the dedication that had carried her this far.

Some of her teachers even nominated her for local youth awards, recognizing her achievements as a young entrepreneur. They saw her growth and were in awe of how she had managed to juggle school with running a successful business. They knew her as more than just a student; Riley had become an inspiration, showing what was possible with dedication, hard work, and a heart committed to positive change.

As Riley walked through the hallways, she felt the weight of her journey. Some of her classmates recognized her as the "ice cream girl," a title that had become part of her identity. Students she barely knew would stop her to congratulate her or ask questions about her business, eager to learn from her experiences. Many of them found encouragement in her story, especially the younger students who hoped to make an impact on their own terms.

Her teachers weren't the only ones inspired by her journey. Younger students had begun looking up to her, viewing her as a role model. She had come to realize that Harvest Creamery was more than just a business; it was a story of resilience and creativity that touched the lives of those around her. Riley was proud to be a source of inspiration, but as graduation approached, she knew there was more she wanted to achieve.

One afternoon, Riley's guidance counselor pulled her aside with a suggestion: apply for college scholarships. At first, Riley felt hesitant. With so much on her plate, she wondered if she had time for another commitment. But the counselor insisted, pointing out that Riley's unique path made her a strong candidate for prestigious scholarships. Her journey, dedication to sustainability, and entrepreneurial achievements could give her an edge in the competitive world of scholarship applications.

With her teachers and counselor's encouragement, Riley decided to go for it. She spent the next few evenings researching universities with strong programs in business, entrepreneurship, and sustainability. She wanted a place that aligned with her values, where she could deepen her knowledge, gain new insights, and bring fresh ideas back to Harvest Creamery.

Late-night essay writing sessions became her new routine. After a full day of school and a few hours managing Harvest Creamery, Riley would sit down with her laptop, pouring her story into each application. In her essays, she reflected on her journey, the obstacles she had overcome, and the values that had shaped her business. She described the day her dream was born in Paris, tasting farm-to-table ice cream for the first time, and how that moment had transformed her life.

As she crafted her narrative, she thought of her partnership with Mr. Stoltzfus and the Amish community. She shared the lessons she had learned from them—the importance of ethical business practices, the beauty of sustainability, and the strength of community support. Each essay became a piece of her heart, a reflection of her growth and the values that had driven her to build something meaningful.

When her essays were complete, Riley's dad offered to help review them. He read through each one carefully, offering feedback and reminding her to keep her voice strong. He wanted her passion for Harvest Creamery and her dedication to her community to shine through in every word. Her teachers also provided glowing letters of recommendation, highlighting her character, work ethic, and the positive impact she had made at school and in the wider community.

Riley's friends rallied behind her, helping her prepare for the interviews that would follow. They transformed her living room into a mock interview space, taking turns asking her questions as they pretended to be members of a scholarship committee. They joked and laughed, but their support meant the world to Riley. It gave her the confidence to walk into each real interview with calm and assurance.

Graduation day crept closer, bringing with it a flood of emotions. Riley had spent four transformative years at John Bowne High, and now she was on the cusp of a new chapter. She felt pride, excitement, and a touch of sadness as she thought about leaving behind the place that had seen her dream grow. Graduation would be a celebration of all she had accomplished, every challenge she had faced, and every victory she had won.

On the morning of graduation, Riley donned her cap and gown, her heart pounding with anticipation. As she walked across the stage to accept her diploma, she saw her parents, friends, and teachers cheering from the audience. Her mom was wiping away tears, her dad was beaming with pride, and her friends were clapping and shouting her name. In that moment, Riley felt a surge of gratitude, knowing that she was surrounded by people who had supported her every step of the way.

To her surprise, the principal invited her to the podium to give a short speech. Riley took a deep breath and stepped forward, her mind racing with memories of her journey. She spoke from the heart, sharing her story with her classmates and thanking her community for their unwavering support. She encouraged her fellow graduates to follow their dreams, to stay true to their values, and to find strength in the people around them.

The audience erupted in applause as she finished, and Riley returned to her seat, feeling a profound sense of fulfillment. Graduation was a milestone, but it was also a beginning—a chapter in a story that was still being written. She knew that her journey was far from over, and that there were still dreams to chase and goals to achieve.

A few weeks after graduation, Riley received an envelope from one of the top universities she had applied to. Her hands shook as she opened it, her heart racing. Inside was a letter congratulating her on being awarded a full scholarship to the university's renowned business program. She gasped, tears filling her eyes as she read the words. She had done it. She had been given an opportunity to continue her education, to learn from experts, and to expand her vision for Harvest Creamery.

Her parents hugged her tightly, their faces filled with pride and joy. Her friends and family celebrated with her, recognizing the scholarship as the culmination of years of hard work and dedication. Riley felt an overwhelming sense of accomplishment, knowing that all her efforts had led her to this moment. The scholarship was more than a reward; it was an opportunity, a responsibility, and a stepping stone toward a future filled with possibilities.

As summer unfolded, Riley began preparing for her transition to university. She spent hours planning for the future of Harvest Creamery, setting up systems to ensure that her team could manage the business while she pursued her studies. She created a schedule of check-ins, set up communication channels, and made sure that her team knew how to handle each aspect of the business.

Her team stepped up eagerly, each member taking on additional responsibilities. The marketing manager crafted new campaigns to keep Harvest Creamery's message alive, the distribution coordinator streamlined the delivery process, and the administrative assistant managed customer inquiries and order fulfillment. Riley was grateful for their dedication, knowing that Harvest Creamery was in good hands.

Leaving her business, family, and friends wasn't easy, but Riley knew that this new chapter was essential for her growth. She felt a mixture of excitement and apprehension as she packed her bags, ready to embark on a journey that would challenge her and expand her horizons. Her parents helped her load her belongings into the car, sharing stories of their own college experiences and reassuring her that they would always be there to support her.

As they drove to the university, Riley looked out the window, her mind filled with memories of the journey that had brought her here. She thought of the Paris trip that had sparked her dream, the partnership with Mr. Stoltzfus, and the community that had rallied behind her vision. She knew that she was leaving behind more than just a business; she was leaving behind a piece of herself, a piece that she would carry with her into this new chapter.

When they arrived on campus, Riley felt a surge of excitement as she took in the bustling atmosphere, the students hurrying to classes, the expansive green lawns, and the towering academic buildings. She knew that this was a new world, one filled with possibilities, challenges, and the chance to learn from some of the best minds in the field. She was ready to face this chapter with the same determination that had fueled her journey so far.

The first few days were a whirlwind of orientation events, meeting new classmates, and exploring the sprawling campus. Riley quickly found her rhythm, balancing her studies with her responsibilities at Harvest Creamery. The courses were challenging, the professors demanding, but Riley was energized by the wealth of knowledge she was gaining. Each lesson, each lecture, felt like another piece of the puzzle, bringing her closer to her dream of expanding her business.

Throughout her time at university, Riley stayed connected to her team, regularly checking in to offer guidance and support. She was proud to see them handling challenges with confidence, their dedication a testament to the values they all shared. Harvest Creamery continued to thrive, its reputation growing even as Riley pursued her education.

In quiet moments, Riley would reflect on her journey, on the people who had supported her, and on the dreams that had led her here. She knew that her story was still unfolding, that there were new chapters waiting to be written and new dreams waiting to be realized. Each day brought new challenges and new opportunities, but Riley was ready to face them all, confident in the foundation she had built and the journey that lay ahead.

As she walked across campus, surrounded by students who each had their own dreams, Riley felt a deep sense of purpose. She had built something meaningful, something that connected her to her family, her community, and her own sense of identity. And with each step forward, she carried the spirit of Harvest Creamery with her, a reminder of the journey that had brought her here and the limitless possibilities that lay ahead.

Chapter 12: National Spotlight

Riley sat at her desk, scrolling through emails, when one message caught her eye. The subject line read: *"National Talk Show Opportunity—Feature on Young Entrepreneurs."* She clicked on it, her curiosity piqued, and read through the email in awe. A well-known television show wanted to feature her on an upcoming segment celebrating young entrepreneurs who were making waves in their industries. They'd heard about her story, her dedication to sustainable practices, and her success with Harvest Creamery. The producers were reaching out to invite her to appear as a guest on the show.

Her heart raced with excitement and nerves. She had seen this show before, watched as influential people and rising stars shared their stories and inspired millions. The thought of stepping onto that stage, of sharing her journey with a national audience, was exhilarating. She felt the weight of the opportunity, but also the pressure. This wasn't just about her; it was about the story of Harvest Creamery, the values it represented, and the community that had supported her from the beginning.

Riley's first instinct was to call her parents. She picked up the phone, dialing their number with shaky hands. When her mom answered, Riley could hardly contain her excitement. "Mom, you won't believe this—I just got an invitation to be on a national talk show. They want to feature Harvest Creamery!"

Her mom let out a gasp, her voice filled with pride and joy. "Riley, that's amazing! This is such a huge opportunity. I'm so proud of you."

Her dad joined the call, equally excited and encouraging. They talked through the details, discussing what this kind of exposure could mean for her business. Her parents reminded her to stay true to herself, to share the heart and soul of Harvest Creamery with the world. Riley knew that this was her chance to tell her story in her own words, to connect with people beyond her community and share the mission that had driven her from the beginning.

The next few days were a whirlwind of preparation. The show's producers arranged for a car service to pick her up and take her to the studio. They explained the process, guiding her through what to expect and offering tips for navigating the on-air interview. Riley spent hours preparing, going over her story and practicing her responses to potential questions. She wanted to make sure that she conveyed the passion behind Harvest Creamery, the dedication to quality, and the importance of supporting local farms and sustainable practices.

The night before the show, Riley could hardly sleep. She lay in bed, her mind racing with thoughts of the interview. She pictured herself on stage, speaking to millions of people, sharing the journey that had brought her here. She thought of the challenges she had faced, the people who had believed in her, and the values that had guided her every step of the way. She reminded herself to stay calm, to trust her instincts, and to let her story speak for itself.

When the day finally arrived, Riley dressed in a simple but elegant outfit, choosing something that made her feel confident and comfortable. As she arrived at the studio, her nerves intensified. The bustling energy of the set, the flashing lights, and the crew members hurrying back and forth all felt overwhelming. She was ushered into a makeup room, where a stylist worked on her hair and makeup, chatting with her and trying to ease her nerves.

The show's producer came by to check in, offering a reassuring smile and a few last-minute tips. "Just be yourself, Riley," she said. "Our viewers are going to love your story. You've got something special to share, so let your passion shine through."

Riley took a deep breath, nodding as she absorbed the producer's words. She reminded herself of her mission, the heart and soul of Harvest Creamery, and the community that had been there from the beginning. She wanted this interview to be a reflection of everything her business stood for, a celebration of the values that had driven her to create something meaningful.

When it was time to go on stage, Riley felt a mixture of excitement and nerves. The host introduced her, sharing a brief summary of her journey and highlighting her success as a young entrepreneur. Riley walked onto the stage, greeted by applause from the audience. She shook hands with the host, taking a seat across from him, her heart pounding with anticipation.

The host began by asking her to share the story behind Harvest Creamery. Riley took a deep breath, letting her nerves settle as she started to speak. She talked about her trip to Paris, the magical experience of tasting farm-to-table ice cream for the first time, and how that moment had sparked her dream. She described her partnership with Mr. Stoltzfus and the Amish community, the values they shared, and the dedication to quality that had become the foundation of her business.

As Riley spoke, the audience listened intently, captivated by her story. She could feel their support, their interest, and it gave her the confidence to keep going. She shared the challenges she had faced, the obstacles she had overcome, and the lessons she had learned along the way. She talked about the importance of supporting local farms, of staying true to one's values, and of building a business that made a positive impact on the world.

The host was clearly impressed, asking thoughtful questions and giving Riley the space to share her story in her own words. He praised her dedication, her resilience, and the way she had turned a dream into a thriving business. He asked about her plans for the future, her vision for expanding Harvest Creamery, and the impact she hoped to make in the world.

Riley answered each question with sincerity and passion, sharing her dreams of growing Harvest Creamery, of reaching more people, and of inspiring other young entrepreneurs to follow their own paths. She talked about the importance of sustainability, of making choices that benefited both people and the planet, and of building a brand that people could trust.

As the interview continued, Riley felt a sense of ease settle over her. She was no longer just a guest on a TV show; she was a storyteller, sharing the journey that had brought her to this moment. She could feel the connection with the audience, a bond that went beyond words. She realized that Harvest Creamery was more than just a business; it was a story that resonated with people, a reminder that dreams were worth pursuing.

When the interview ended, the audience erupted in applause, and Riley felt a surge of pride and gratitude. She had done it. She had shared her story with the world, and she could feel the impact of her words. As she left the stage, the show's crew congratulated her, each one offering words of encouragement and admiration.

Back in the dressing room, Riley checked her phone, and she was overwhelmed by the flood of messages and notifications. Friends, family, and customers had all watched the interview, each one sending messages of support and pride. Her social media accounts were buzzing with new followers, each one eager to learn more about Harvest Creamery and the story behind it.

The impact of the interview was immediate. Orders for her ice cream began pouring in from across the country, people reaching out to try the flavors that had captured their imaginations. Riley's team back in Bayside was working around the clock to keep up with the demand, the excitement of the national spotlight fueling their energy.

Riley quickly realized that the interview had brought Harvest Creamery to a whole new level. She was no longer just a local entrepreneur; she was a national sensation, her story resonating with people from coast to coast. She felt the weight of the responsibility, but also the thrill of the opportunity. This was her chance to make a difference, to expand her reach, and to share her values with a larger audience.

Her phone rang, and it was her dad. "Riley, you were amazing. We're so proud of you," he said, his voice filled with pride. Riley thanked him, feeling a surge of gratitude for the family and community that had supported her every step of the way.

In the days that followed, Riley's life changed in ways she hadn't anticipated. She received invitations from other media outlets, each one eager to share her story. She was featured in articles, interviewed by journalists, and celebrated as a young entrepreneur who was making a positive impact on the world. Her inbox was filled with messages from people who had been inspired by her journey, each one sharing their own dreams and thanking her for showing them what was possible.

The sudden fame was exhilarating, but it also brought new challenges. Riley had to navigate the demands of media attention, balancing her responsibilities at Harvest Creamery with the new opportunities that came her way. She was constantly on the go, meeting with potential partners, coordinating with her team, and planning for the future.

Her team stepped up to the challenge, each member playing a crucial role in managing the surge of new orders and inquiries. They worked tirelessly, their dedication a testament to the values that had built Harvest Creamery. The office in Bayside became a hive of activity, each person contributing their skills and energy to keep the business running smoothly.

Despite the whirlwind of attention, Riley remained grounded in her mission. She knew that the heart of Harvest Creamery was its commitment to quality, sustainability, and community. She reminded herself to stay true to her values, to let her passion guide her decisions, and to focus on making a positive impact.

As the weeks went by, Riley settled into her new role as a national figure. She embraced the opportunities that came her way, each one a chance to share her story and inspire others. She continued to work closely with her team, ensuring that Harvest Creamery maintained its dedication to quality and sustainability even as it grew.

Through it all, Riley felt a deep sense of gratitude. She knew that her journey had been shaped by the people who had believed in her, the community that had supported her, and the values that had guided her from the beginning. The national spotlight was thrilling, but it was also a reminder of the responsibility she held—to her customers, her team, and the world around her.

Riley's journey from a young girl with a dream to a national sensation was a testament to the power of resilience, passion, and authenticity. She knew that the road ahead would be filled with new challenges, but she was ready to face them with confidence and determination. Each day brought new opportunities, new reasons to be grateful, and new ways to make a difference.

As she looked out over the bustling office, surrounded by her team and the fruits of her labor, Riley felt a deep sense of fulfillment. She had built something meaningful, something that connected her to her community, her family, and her own sense of purpose. Each step of the journey had brought her closer to her dreams, and with each new opportunity, she was reminded of the limitless possibilities that lay ahead.

Chapter 13: Success and Struggles

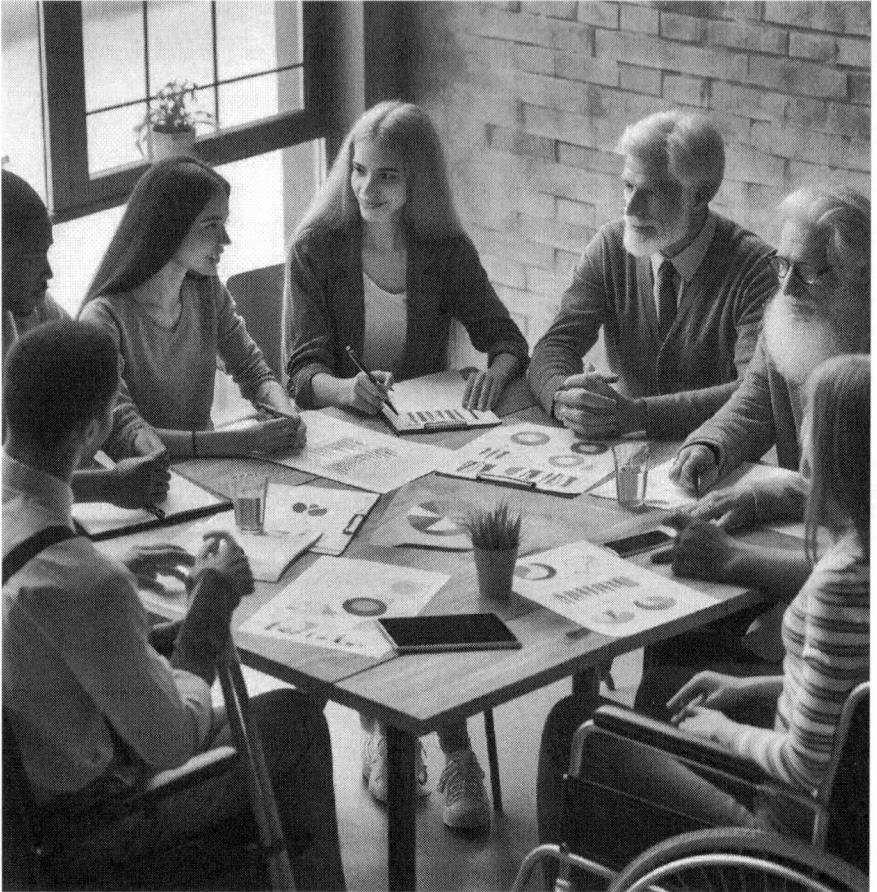

Riley had always dreamed of Harvest Creamery's success, but she had never anticipated the sheer intensity of life in the spotlight. Since her television appearance, her business had soared to new heights. Orders flooded in, partnerships blossomed, and her inbox overflowed with emails from journalists, customers, and fellow entrepreneurs. It was exhilarating to see her brand on the national stage, her story inspiring people across the country. But with the newfound fame came unexpected challenges.

She quickly found herself pulled in multiple directions. Media requests piled up, each one eager to capture the story behind Harvest Creamery. Business partners, both new and old, reached out with proposals, and her schedule filled with meetings, interviews, and events. Riley felt like she was always running, her days packed with calls, strategy sessions, and planning meetings. The business was thriving, but the pressure was overwhelming.

Her team noticed the shift too. The office had become a hive of constant activity, each person managing a growing list of responsibilities. Riley's marketing manager was working overtime, fielding media inquiries and managing social media. Her distribution coordinator scrambled to meet the surge in demand, organizing shipments to new retail locations across the country. Everyone was stretched thin, but they pushed forward, fueled by the excitement of Harvest Creamery's success.

As the business continued to expand, Riley realized that she was losing touch with the simple joy that had once defined her journey. Her days became a blur of deadlines and obligations, leaving her little time to connect with her team, her family, or herself. She missed the early days, the quiet moments in her garage where she had crafted each flavor with care. Now, her hands rarely touched the ingredients; she was too busy managing the endless stream of responsibilities.

One afternoon, Riley's parents invited her over for a family dinner, hoping to spend some time with her amidst her hectic schedule. As she sat at the table, listening to their familiar voices, she felt a pang of longing for the simple, grounded life she had once known. Her parents noticed her exhaustion, the way her smile seemed forced, her eyes tired. They asked her about the business, about how she was holding up with all the new demands.

Riley hesitated, struggling to find the words to express the whirlwind she was caught in. "It's amazing, but it's... a lot," she admitted, her voice barely above a whisper. She shared the pressure she felt, the overwhelming sense of responsibility to keep up with the demand, and the weight of being in the public eye. Her parents listened patiently, offering words of encouragement and reminding her of the importance of balance.

Her mom placed a gentle hand on hers. "Riley, you've accomplished so much, but don't forget to take care of yourself. You're more than your business. Make sure you're finding time for the things that bring you joy."

The words struck a chord with Riley. She realized that she had been so focused on building Harvest Creamery that she had neglected her own well-being. She was constantly on the go, pushing herself to meet every expectation, but she had lost touch with the joy that had once fueled her passion. She left that dinner feeling both comforted and unsettled, the realization of her own exhaustion settling heavily on her shoulders.

In the following weeks, Riley made an effort to slow down, to carve out moments of rest amidst the chaos. She started small, taking short breaks during the day to clear her mind, to step outside and breathe. She began setting boundaries, limiting the number of interviews and meetings she accepted, allowing herself the space to recharge. It wasn't easy—her instinct was to say yes to every opportunity, to push forward without stopping—but she knew that she couldn't sustain her pace without burning out.

As she focused on self-care, Riley discovered a newfound sense of resilience. She learned that rest wasn't a sign of weakness, but a crucial part of maintaining her strength. She realized that she didn't have to do everything alone, that her team was there to support her, to carry the weight when she needed to step back. Slowly, she began to let go of the need for control, trusting her team to handle their responsibilities with the same care and dedication that she brought to her work.

The change wasn't immediate, but it was profound. Riley began to find joy in her work again, rediscovering the passion that had first driven her to create Harvest Creamery. She reconnected with her team, taking time to listen to their ideas, to celebrate their successes, and to share in the journey they were building together. The office felt different—a little more grounded, a little more connected, as everyone worked together with a renewed sense of purpose.

Riley's journey of self-care extended beyond the office. She reconnected with her friends, who had been there from the beginning, the ones who had cheered her on through every challenge. They became her anchor, a reminder of the simple joys and laughter that had once filled her days. She made time for coffee dates, for movie nights, for the moments of connection that reminded her of who she was beyond her business.

One evening, Riley's best friend invited her to a small gathering, a chance to relax and unwind with people who knew her before Harvest Creamery's success. They sat around a fire, sharing stories, laughing, and reminiscing about the early days. Riley felt a sense of peace settle over her, a reminder that she was more than her accomplishments. She was a daughter, a friend, a young woman with dreams that went beyond business.

The friendships she had nurtured over the years became a source of strength, each one a reminder of the importance of balance. Her friends understood her struggles, her moments of doubt, and they offered unwavering support. They reminded her to find joy in the journey, to celebrate the small victories, and to take pride in the person she had become.

As Riley navigated the complexities of her new life, she learned invaluable lessons about resilience, about the strength that came from within. She discovered that true success wasn't just about achievements; it was about the journey, the people who walked alongside her, and the moments of growth that shaped her. She realized that she didn't have to have all the answers, that it was okay to ask for help, to lean on others when the weight felt too heavy.

Through her struggles, Riley found a new sense of clarity. She redefined her vision for Harvest Creamery, focusing not just on growth, but on the values that had driven her from the beginning. She wanted her business to be a reflection of the things she believed in—authenticity, community, and the joy of creating something meaningful. She shared this vision with her team, each one resonating with her words, inspired by her commitment to building a business that was more than just a brand.

Together, they worked to bring this vision to life, each person contributing their unique skills and perspectives. They launched new initiatives that emphasized sustainability, that highlighted their partnerships with local farmers, and that celebrated the people who made Harvest Creamery possible. The business became a true reflection of their collective values, a brand that people trusted, not just for its products, but for its purpose.

Riley's journey wasn't without its setbacks. She faced moments of doubt, times when the pressure felt overwhelming, but she learned to embrace these challenges as opportunities for growth. Each obstacle became a lesson, a reminder of the strength that lay within her. She realized that resilience wasn't just about pushing through; it was about adapting, about finding new ways to navigate the path ahead.

In time, Riley became a mentor to other young entrepreneurs, each one inspired by her journey and eager to learn from her experiences. She shared her story openly, the struggles and the successes, the moments of doubt and the triumphs. She wanted to be a source of support, a reminder that success wasn't a straight line, that it was filled with twists and turns, each one a chance to learn and grow.

Riley's life had changed in ways she hadn't anticipated, but through it all, she remained true to herself. She had built something meaningful, something that connected her to her community, to her family, and to her own sense of purpose. Each day brought new challenges, but also new reasons to be grateful, new moments of joy and connection.

Chapter 14: Financial Foundations

Riley sat in her office, reviewing her latest financial statements. The numbers told a story of growth, hard work, and a touch of magic. Harvest Creamery's revenue had soared into the millions—a testament to the dedication and passion she'd poured into her business. While the success was thrilling, it also brought with it new responsibilities. Managing a growing enterprise required Riley to make decisions not only about the future of her business but also about her personal finances.

As she looked over the reports, she felt the weight of the decisions ahead. She had built Harvest Creamery with care, and now she wanted to ensure that her finances were just as thoughtfully managed. She had heard stories of successful entrepreneurs who had lost fortunes due to poor financial planning, and she was determined to avoid those pitfalls. Riley wanted to create a secure foundation that would support her personal goals and ensure Harvest Creamery's stability.

Sitting down with her parents that evening, Riley shared her thoughts. "I'm grateful for everything that's happening, but I feel like I'm in uncharted territory," she said. "I've never managed this kind of money, and I want to make sure I'm making the right choices."

Her father nodded, understanding her concerns. "You've done an incredible job building Harvest Creamery," he said. "But managing wealth at this level is complex. I think it's time for you to speak with a professional financial advisor—someone who can guide you in making sound investment decisions and help you secure what you've worked so hard to build."

The idea resonated with Riley. She had always sought knowledge and guidance from trusted sources, and this felt like the next logical step. She realized that managing finances on this scale required specialized knowledge, and she wanted to approach it thoughtfully. However, she knew that the journey to finding the right advisor would be one she'd undertake carefully.

After spending time researching financial advisors in her area, reading testimonials, and consulting friends, she arranged consultations with several highly recommended, certified financial advisors. Riley wanted to work with someone who understood her values and could offer her suggestions on wealth management without pushing her in any particular direction. She recognized the importance of diverse perspectives, so she met with three different advisors, each bringing a unique approach.

Each consultation introduced her to new concepts and strategies. While Riley appreciated each advisor's perspective, she was careful to gather information and assess the options herself. The third advisor she met with, Mark Palmer, stood out to her for his straightforward approach and deep experience working with young entrepreneurs. She felt an immediate sense of trust with Mark, who respected her goals and understood the challenges of managing wealth at her stage in life.

It's worth noting that financial strategies vary based on individual goals, risk tolerance, and circumstances. For readers considering their own financial plans, it's crucial to consult a qualified financial advisor, tax professional, or legal expert. Laws and tax implications differ widely, and a financial strategy that works well for one person may not suit another. Professional guidance ensures that each decision aligns with one's financial goals, risk tolerance, and legal obligations. Riley's story here is purely a narrative exploration of her journey into financial literacy, intended to illustrate the learning process involved in wealth management and is fictional.

When Riley met with Mark, she knew she was not committing to any specific plan but rather learning about various options available to her. Their first meeting was introductory, with Mark explaining general principles of financial planning. He outlined the importance of diversification, spreading her investments across different asset types to minimize risk. Riley appreciated the way he simplified complex ideas, helping her understand how each asset could contribute to a balanced portfolio.

Mark's role was to offer suggestions, giving Riley an array of choices to consider. He emphasized that the ultimate decision would be hers, shaped by her risk tolerance, goals, and values. "My job is to give you the tools and information you need to make decisions," he said. "I'll present some options, and you can decide what feels right for you."

Mark began by explaining the basics of stocks, which represent partial ownership in companies. He suggested that stocks could offer her the potential for growth over time but were more volatile than some other assets. "The stock market can be unpredictable," he explained, "but investing in stable, well-established companies can reduce some of that risk. These companies are called 'blue-chip' stocks—high-quality businesses with strong financial histories."

Riley was intrigued by the idea of investing in companies that aligned with her values. Mark introduced her to the concept of ESG (Environmental, Social, and Governance) investing, where investors choose companies committed to ethical and sustainable practices. Riley appreciated the concept and felt it resonated with the values that had guided her in building Harvest Creamery.

However, Mark was careful to clarify that ESG stocks might not always provide the highest returns compared to other options. Still, they could potentially provide steady growth and align with Riley's commitment to social responsibility. He suggested a few well-regarded ESG companies, letting her decide whether this approach suited her objectives. He reminded her that each option was simply a suggestion, not a recommendation.

They moved on to discuss another type of investment—Exchange-Traded Funds, or ETFs. Mark described ETFs as bundles of stocks or bonds that trade on the market like individual stocks. "ETFs can be a great way to diversify," he explained. "For example, instead of buying individual stocks, you could purchase an ETF that represents a basket of stocks in a particular industry, like clean energy or technology."

Riley liked the idea of ETFs because they allowed her to invest in multiple companies at once, spreading her risk. Mark recommended a few ETFs that focused on sectors relevant to her interests, like sustainable industries and technology. He emphasized that ETFs allowed her to diversify without the need for constant monitoring, as they were often managed by investment professionals. Riley saw the appeal of ETFs and decided to add them to her list of potential investments.

Mark then introduced her to bonds, which he described as loans she could make to companies or governments in exchange for regular interest payments. Bonds, he explained, were generally less volatile than stocks, providing a steady, predictable income. "With bonds, you're essentially lending money, with the promise that it will be repaid with interest," he said. "They offer stability, and they can be an anchor in your portfolio."

Mark discussed the two primary types of bonds Riley might consider: corporate and municipal bonds. Corporate bonds were issued by companies and tended to offer higher interest rates, but they came with more risk. Municipal bonds, on the other hand, were issued by local governments and often provided tax-free income. "For someone looking for stability and a predictable income stream, bonds can be an excellent choice," he explained, letting her weigh the options.

They also discussed laddering, a bond strategy where she could stagger the maturity dates, creating a steady stream of income as each bond matured. This approach would provide her with regular funds to reinvest, ensuring that her portfolio remained active and adaptable. Riley saw the practicality of laddering, appreciating the steady income it would generate.

Mark introduced Riley to alternative assets she could explore further if she wanted. He mentioned TIPS, or Treasury Inflation-Protected Securities, which are government bonds designed to protect against inflation. Mark explained that TIPS paid interest like traditional bonds, but their principal increased with inflation, providing a safeguard against the rising cost of living.

Riley appreciated the idea of TIPS, especially in an uncertain economic climate. She knew inflation could impact her purchasing power over time, so the concept of inflation-protected bonds felt appealing. Mark carefully explained that TIPS offered security but generally had lower returns than other investment options. He emphasized that they were an option to consider, and she could make a final decision after more research.

Throughout the discussions, Mark emphasized that he was not making recommendations but rather offering a range of strategies and tools. Riley understood that each suggestion came with its own risks and benefits, and she would need to carefully evaluate each option before making any decisions.

As they wrapped up their series of meetings, Riley felt more empowered and informed. Her financial knowledge had expanded, and she began to see how different investment instruments could work together in a diversified portfolio. Stocks could offer growth, bonds could provide stability, ETFs could add diversification, and TIPS could serve as a layer of inflation protection.

Before making any final decisions, Riley consulted additional certified advisors to gather different perspectives on her financial plan. She met with tax professionals and legal experts to fully understand the implications of each investment choice. Each consultation added another layer to her understanding, helping her approach her financial journey with confidence.

Through this journey, Riley realized the importance of financial literacy. She understood that professional advice was crucial to making informed choices and that each investment decision carried its own set of responsibilities. By consulting multiple advisors, she felt she had equipped herself with a broad foundation of knowledge.

With her financial plan in place, Riley felt a newfound sense of stability and readiness. She knew that her wealth was protected and strategically positioned for the future. This journey had taught her the value of informed decision-making, the importance of professional guidance, and the peace of mind that came from a well-structured financial plan.

Chapter 15: A Sweet New Chapter

Riley couldn't shake the idea of doing something bold, something that would add a new layer of excitement to Harvest Creamery's lineup. Her ice cream was already loved by customers across the east coast, but she craved an expansion that would spark even more enthusiasm. She wanted to create a product that would take her brand to the next level—a dessert that celebrated both the artistry of her ingredients and the joy of shared moments.

One evening, as she mulled over ideas, an old memory drifted into her mind: her family gathering around a beautifully decorated ice cream cake for her 10th birthday. She could almost taste the layers of ice cream and cake, the richness of the flavors that made each bite feel like a celebration. It was that very sensation she wanted to bring to her customers, to create something that wasn't just a dessert but an experience.

Excited, Riley quickly jotted down her thoughts. She wanted Harvest Creamery's ice cream cakes to feel nostalgic yet fresh, like a tribute to those cherished family gatherings but elevated with the quality and authenticity her brand was known for. She envisioned beautifully layered cakes that would blend flavors, textures, and colors in a way that felt unique, vibrant, and completely true to Harvest Creamery's philosophy.

The next morning, she called a team meeting, brimming with ideas. Her team gathered around, listening intently as she explained her vision. "I want us to create ice cream cakes that feel special," Riley said, her eyes alight with excitement. "I'm talking about cakes that tell a story with each bite—something that reminds people of celebrations but with the Harvest Creamery touch."

Her marketing manager, Heather, immediately saw the potential. "Riley, this is incredible! Ice cream cakes are a classic, but we could bring something totally unique to the market. Imagine the impact of cakes with flavors that reflect the seasons, each one crafted with local ingredients."

Marco, her head chef and product developer, was equally enthusiastic. "We could experiment with different combinations—layered cakes with flavors that complement each other perfectly. There's so much we can do to make these cakes extraordinary." He began brainstorming out loud, throwing out ideas for flavors, fillings, and textures.

Riley's heart swelled as she watched her team rally around the idea, their minds racing with possibilities. She knew they were on the verge of something special, something that would capture the essence of Harvest Creamery while also expanding its reach. Ice cream cakes could open up new doors, attracting a whole new audience and giving existing customers a reason to celebrate.

The first step was research. Riley and her team spent days studying the ice cream cake market, analyzing popular trends, and exploring what other brands were offering. They ordered cakes from local bakeries, gourmet stores, and high-end brands, taking notes on flavors, textures, and presentation. Each tasting session was a chance to learn, to identify what worked and what didn't, and to think about how they could set Harvest Creamery's cakes apart.

One thing became clear: they needed a unique angle. While most ice cream cakes were either overly sweet or laden with artificial ingredients, Riley wanted hers to reflect Harvest Creamery's farm-to-table ethos. She wanted each cake to feel like a handcrafted work of art, made with the same fresh, seasonal ingredients that defined her ice cream.

Riley and her team moved on to the most exciting part of the project—developing the actual flavors. Marco took charge of the kitchen, transforming it into a hub of creativity and experimentation. They worked with seasonal ingredients, drawing inspiration from local farms, orchards, and gardens. Riley wanted each cake to celebrate the flavors of nature, to be as much a feast for the eyes as for the taste buds.

The first cake they tackled was a caramel apple ice cream cake. They layered spiced apple compote with creamy caramel ice cream, adding a hint of cinnamon and nutmeg for warmth. Marco experimented with different textures, incorporating a layer of graham cracker crust for crunch and a swirl of honey caramel that added depth and richness. The cake felt like autumn on a plate—a reminder of apple picking and crisp fall days.

Next came a summer berry cake, a tribute to the vibrant flavors of the season. Riley and Marco created layers of blueberry, strawberry, and raspberry ice creams, each one bursting with the freshness of ripe berries. They added a layer of vanilla sponge cake, soft and light, that brought the flavors together. The cake was a colorful masterpiece, each slice revealing a rainbow of reds, blues, and purples that celebrated the bounty of summer.

The final flavor in their core lineup was a decadent chocolate hazelnut cake, perfect for those who craved something rich and indulgent. Marco crafted layers of chocolate and hazelnut ice creams, adding a swirl of dark chocolate fudge in the center. The cake was finished with a layer of chocolate ganache, smooth and glossy, and topped with a sprinkle of roasted hazelnuts. It was a luxurious dessert, each bite a blend of creamy, crunchy, and deeply satisfying flavors.

Riley and her team tasted each creation, savoring the balance of flavors, textures, and colors. Each cake felt like a reflection of Harvest Creamery's values, a celebration of quality ingredients and careful craftsmanship. They knew they had something special, something that would resonate with customers and offer a new way to experience the brand.

With the flavors set, Riley turned her attention to branding. She wanted the ice cream cakes to have their own unique identity while still feeling connected to the Harvest Creamery family. Heather worked with a local designer to create a logo for the new line, something simple and elegant that conveyed the artistry of the cakes. They chose soft, earthy colors for the packaging—creams, greens, and browns—that reflected the natural beauty of the ingredients.

The branding extended to the names of the cakes as well. Heather came up with the idea of naming each cake after the inspiration behind it. The caramel apple cake became "The Orchard," a tribute to the apple orchards that supplied their ingredients. The berry cake was named "Summer's Bounty," a celebration of the farms that provided the berries. The chocolate hazelnut cake was christened "The Harvest," a nod to the richness of the ingredients and the abundance of nature.

With the branding complete, it was time to think about the launch. Riley wanted the introduction of the ice cream cakes to feel like a celebration, a chance to connect with customers and share the journey that had brought them here. They decided to host a launch event at the farm, inviting local influencers, media, and loyal customers to be the first to experience the new cakes. It would be a day of tastings, tours, and storytelling, a way to introduce the cakes in a setting that reflected Harvest Creamery's values.

On the day of the event, the farm was transformed into a picturesque venue. Tables were set with beautiful displays of each cake flavor, the layers visible through glass cake stands that highlighted the colors and textures. Riley had decorated the space with fresh flowers, fruits, and greenery, each detail chosen to reflect the natural beauty of the ingredients.

Guests arrived with excitement, greeted by the inviting aroma of freshly prepared cake samples. They moved from table to table, tasting each flavor, marveling at the balance and artistry of the cakes. Riley watched as people's faces lit up with delight, their expressions a mix of surprise and joy as they tasted the carefully crafted flavors. The feedback was overwhelmingly positive, each guest praising the quality, the creativity, and the connection to the land.

Throughout the event, Riley shared the story behind each cake, talking to guests about the inspiration, the ingredients, and the process of bringing her vision to life. She felt a deep sense of pride as she watched people connect with the cakes, each bite a testament to the dedication and care that had gone into their creation. It was a moment of fulfillment, a reminder of why she had started Harvest Creamery in the first place.

The launch was a success, and by the end of the day, orders were already coming in for the ice cream cakes. Riley and her team were thrilled, but they also realized the challenges that lay ahead. The demand for the cakes was higher than they had anticipated, and they needed to find a way to keep up without compromising the quality that defined their brand.

Riley began working closely with her advisors to develop a plan for scaling production sustainably. They discussed options for expanding the kitchen, hiring additional staff, and investing in equipment that would streamline the process without sacrificing the artisan quality of the cakes. Each decision was made carefully, with a commitment to preserving the heart of Harvest Creamery.

The journey wasn't without its setbacks. As they navigated the complexities of scaling, Riley faced moments of doubt, times when the pressure felt overwhelming. But through it all, she remained focused on her vision, on the values that had brought her this far. She leaned on her team, trusting their expertise and encouraging them to bring their ideas to the table.

As the weeks went by, Riley found herself learning new lessons about resilience, innovation, and leadership. She discovered that success wasn't just about creating something beautiful; it was about sustaining it, about finding ways to grow without losing the soul of the business. She learned to adapt, to embrace the challenges, and to view each obstacle as an opportunity for growth.

The popularity of the ice cream cakes continued to grow, reaching customers far beyond their initial audience. Social media buzzed with photos of the cakes, each post a celebration of the flavors, the artistry, and the Harvest Creamery philosophy. Customers ordered cakes for birthdays, weddings, and special occasions, each one a reminder of the joy that food could bring.

Riley's journey from inspiration to execution, from concept to completion, was a testament to her dedication, her creativity, and her commitment to quality. The ice cream cakes had become more than just a new product; they were a chapter in the story of Harvest Creamery, a reflection of the values that had built the brand.

Through the ups and downs, the triumphs and challenges, Riley remained focused on her mission. She knew that each decision she made, each cake she crafted, was a part of something bigger, a legacy that celebrated the beauty of food, the power of community, and the joy of shared moments.

Chapter 16: Giving Back

As Harvest Creamery continued to grow and her financial foundation strengthened, Riley found herself reflecting on the journey that had brought her to this moment. She had been incredibly fortunate, supported by her family, mentors, and community as she built her business from the ground up. But now, with her business thriving, Riley felt a calling to give back. She wanted to use her success not just to elevate her own life but to make a meaningful difference for others.

The idea of giving back had been in her mind for a while, but she wasn't quite sure where to start. Philanthropy was more than just writing a check—it was about creating opportunities, empowering others, and making a lasting impact. She wanted her efforts to align with the values that had always guided Harvest Creamery: authenticity, sustainability, and community.

Sitting down one evening with her parents, Riley shared her vision for the future. "I want to help people who might not have had the same opportunities I did," she said. "I've been so fortunate to have mentors, family, and resources to support me, but not everyone has those advantages. I want to make a real difference for people who are struggling."

Her father smiled, pride evident in his eyes. "Riley, you've always been about more than just success for yourself. Giving back is a beautiful goal, and with everything you've built, I know you'll find a way to make an impact." Her mother nodded in agreement, adding, "Whatever you choose to do, let it be a reflection of who you are. Share the lessons you've learned and show others how to find strength in themselves."

Inspired by their encouragement, Riley began to research different ways she could give back. She considered various avenues for her philanthropy, from scholarships and educational programs to small business support initiatives. After a few weeks of brainstorming, she decided on a dual approach: she would focus on supporting young entrepreneurs and providing resources for low-income communities to access education and basic needs.

One of Riley's core beliefs was that education could be transformative. She wanted to empower people to seek knowledge, skills, and resources that would allow them to improve their lives. She knew that with the right guidance, others could experience the same kind of growth and self-discovery that had fueled her own journey.

Her first step was to establish a foundation through Harvest Creamery, one that would allow her to channel funds into initiatives that aligned with her values. The foundation would focus on three main areas: supporting youth entrepreneurship, funding educational programs, and providing resources to underserved communities. It was a big step, but Riley was committed to making a difference, and she wanted to ensure that every dollar made a meaningful impact.

To get started, Riley reached out to local nonprofits and community organizations to understand the specific needs in her area. She spent weeks meeting with community leaders, educators, and nonprofit directors, listening to their stories and learning about the challenges they faced. Each conversation opened her eyes to the struggles many people experienced, from limited access to education to a lack of basic necessities.

One of the nonprofit directors she met, Linda, ran an organization that provided mentorship and resources for low-income youth. Linda's passion for her work was evident as she described the impact her organization had made in young people's lives. "For a lot of these kids, having someone believe in them is life-changing," Linda explained. "Many of them don't have the support they need at home, and they struggle to envision a brighter future."

Riley felt deeply moved by Linda's words. She knew firsthand the power of mentorship, of having someone to believe in you when times were tough. She decided that her foundation's first initiative would focus on creating a youth entrepreneurship program. This program would provide mentorship, workshops, and funding opportunities for young people interested in starting their own businesses. She wanted to show them that with hard work, dedication, and the right guidance, they could turn their ideas into reality.

Working closely with Linda, Riley designed the youth entrepreneurship program to be accessible and inclusive. The program would offer a series of workshops on topics like business planning, marketing, and financial literacy, each one led by successful entrepreneurs and community leaders. Participants would be paired with mentors who could provide ongoing support, helping them navigate the challenges of starting a business.

The launch of the program was a success. Riley felt a surge of pride as she watched the first group of participants walk through the doors, their faces filled with excitement and curiosity. She spent time talking to each of them, listening to their dreams and aspirations, and sharing her own story. She wanted them to know that she had been in their shoes once, that her journey had started with a simple idea and a lot of determination.

As the program progressed, Riley saw the transformative power of mentorship and education in action. Participants grew in confidence, developed business ideas, and learned skills they could apply not only to entrepreneurship but to all areas of their lives. One young woman, Mia, shared how the program had changed her perspective. "I used to think starting a business was impossible for someone like me," Mia said. "But now, I feel like I have the tools and support to actually make it happen."

Encouraged by the success of the youth entrepreneurship program, Riley turned her attention to education for low-income communities. She wanted to create a program that provided resources and support to students who struggled with access to education. Working with local schools and nonprofits, Riley developed a scholarship fund for students in underserved areas, one that would cover tuition, books, and other essential expenses.

The scholarship fund was launched with great anticipation, and applications poured in from students eager to pursue their education. Riley was moved by the stories that came with each application, stories of resilience, hope, and dreams for a better future. She read each one carefully, reminded of the power of education and the opportunities it could open.

In addition to scholarships, Riley's foundation began funding literacy programs and after-school tutoring for students in underserved communities. She knew that education was not just about college degrees; it was about providing children with the tools they needed to succeed in all aspects of life. The programs quickly gained popularity, and Riley received heartfelt letters from students and parents expressing their gratitude.

One mother wrote, "My son was struggling in school, but with the tutoring program, he's finally starting to catch up. Thank you for helping him find hope and confidence." Another student shared, "Before the program, I didn't think college was possible for me. Now, I have a scholarship, and I'm working hard to make my dreams come true."

The feedback reaffirmed Riley's commitment to her mission. She was making a real difference, and each success story inspired her to keep pushing forward. She continued meeting with community leaders, learning more about the specific needs in each area, and adapting her programs to provide the most effective support.

Beyond financial assistance, Riley felt a responsibility to educate people about the importance of seeking help and resources. She had learned so much from her own mentors and advisors, and she wanted others to know that they, too, could benefit from guidance. She organized a series of community workshops focused on financial literacy, personal growth, and goal setting. These workshops were open to anyone, free of charge, and aimed to empower individuals to take control of their futures.

Riley spoke at several of the workshops, sharing her journey and the lessons she had learned along the way. She emphasized the importance of seeking education, asking questions, and building a support network. "You don't have to go through life alone," she told the audience. "There are people and resources available to help you reach your goals, but you have to be willing to seek them out."

The response was overwhelming. People from all walks of life attended the workshops, each one eager to learn, grow, and improve their lives. Riley felt a deep sense of fulfillment as she watched people leave the sessions with new knowledge and a renewed sense of hope. She knew that education was one of the most powerful tools she could offer, and she was committed to making it accessible to as many people as possible.

Through her foundation, Riley continued to expand her efforts, partnering with organizations across the country to support a range of causes. She funded job training programs, provided grants for small businesses, and supported mental health initiatives in low-income communities. Each project was a reflection of her belief in the potential of every individual, a reminder that with the right support, people could achieve extraordinary things.

Riley's philanthropy efforts transformed her perspective on success. She realized that her greatest achievements weren't measured in profits or accolades but in the lives she was able to touch. She had built something meaningful, something that connected her to her community, her family, and her own sense of purpose.

As she looked back on her journey, Riley felt a profound sense of gratitude for the support she had received along the way. She knew that none of her success would have been possible without the guidance of her mentors, the encouragement of her family, and the resilience of her community. Now, it was her turn to be that source of support for others, to help them find strength, courage, and hope.

Her commitment to giving back became a guiding principle in her life, a reminder of the impact one person could make. With each new initiative, Riley was reminded of the power of kindness, the beauty of community, and the limitless potential of the human spirit. She had found her true calling—not just as an entrepreneur but as a force for good, a beacon of hope for those who needed it most.

Riley's story was a testament to the belief that success meant little without a commitment to helping others. Each day, she felt more fulfilled, more connected to her purpose, and more determined to make a difference.

Chapter 17: The Ice Cream from the Queens Girl

Riley leaned against the rooftop railing, gazing out over New York City. The lights of Queens sparkled beneath her, a landscape she knew so well yet saw with renewed wonder each time she took in the view. It was the city that had raised her, the community that had rooted for her, and now, the place where her dream had grown into a thriving business. She still couldn't quite believe it—Harvest Creamery, the ice cream brand she had started as a teenager, was now known across New York City and along the East Coast. And to think, all of this had started with a single scoop of farm-fresh ice cream in Paris.

This success, though thrilling, was only the beginning. Riley had a clear sense of purpose and drive, and even as her brand grew, her dreams were expanding too. Next year, she would be starting university on a full scholarship, pursuing her studies while managing her business. It was a challenge, but Riley had always thrived on hard work and dedication. University would open doors to new knowledge, skills, and resources that she could bring back to Harvest Creamery. She was determined to grow her business and continue her education, balancing both worlds with the same passion and determination that had brought her this far.

Since her national TV appearance, word of her unique, farm-to-table ice cream had spread across the city. Restaurants, cafes, and local markets proudly featured Harvest Creamery, showcasing the handcrafted, locally sourced products that had made her brand famous. Customers lined up for a taste, eagerly anticipating the seasonal flavors and small-batch creativity that defined Harvest Creamery. Riley's ice cream wasn't just a dessert—it was an experience, a connection to quality ingredients, and a reminder of the community that had supported her dream.

The nickname "The Ice Cream Queen of Queens" had started in the local press, but soon everyone seemed to be calling her that. Riley found herself smiling each time she heard it. It wasn't just a testament to her business; it was a reflection of her roots, of the neighborhood that had believed in her long before her brand became popular. She was proud to represent Queens, to give back to the place that had been her home and her inspiration from the very beginning.

Inside Harvest Creamery's bustling headquarters, the walls were adorned with photos of her journey. There were snapshots of her earliest days, memories from the first batches she'd made in her family kitchen, her trips to the Amish farms to source her ingredients, and her first taste-testing sessions at the local farmers' market. Each image captured a chapter in her story, a reminder of the hard work and faith it had taken to get here. This success wasn't hers alone—it was shared by her family, her friends, her mentors, and her community.

Her team had been with her through it all, many of them starting as volunteers, part-timers, or friends who believed in her vision. Now they were part of a close-knit group that felt more like family than employees. Together, they celebrated Harvest Creamery's growth and success. They shared her values of authenticity, quality, and connection, and they worked tirelessly to ensure each scoop, each batch, and each flavor met the high standards that had set her brand apart. Riley felt immense pride in her team and appreciated the support they provided, especially as she prepared to balance university with her growing responsibilities at Harvest Creamery.

With her acceptance letter in hand and a scholarship secured, Riley knew her next chapter was just beginning. University would provide new perspectives and introduce her to people who could help her bring fresh ideas to Harvest Creamery. She was thrilled about the opportunity to study business and sustainability, fields that would allow her to deepen her understanding of her industry and enhance her brand's mission. But as excited as she was to embark on this new journey, she knew she would always stay connected to her business, managing it remotely and through her dedicated team.

One afternoon, Riley sat down with her head chef, Marco, to discuss the future of Harvest Creamery and the potential for new flavors. Marco had been with her since the start, sharing her vision and passion for innovation. Together, they brainstormed ideas that would keep their offerings fresh and exciting. Marco suggested a "Maple Pecan Pie" flavor, inspired by his grandmother's recipe. They imagined a blend of creamy maple ice cream, caramelized pecans, and buttery pie crust— a flavor that would evoke the warmth of autumn and family traditions.

Riley, in turn, shared an idea she'd been holding onto since Paris: a rose flower, honey blend that would remind customers of the fields and flowers of the French countryside. It felt like a full-circle moment, a way to bring a piece of that transformative experience back to her customers. As they exchanged ideas, Riley's excitement grew. She could see the potential for new flavors and seasonal specials, each one reflecting her journey and the people who had inspired her along the way.

As the meeting wrapped up, Marco asked about her plans for university. He knew she would be managing a full schedule of classes, assignments, and new experiences. Riley smiled, acknowledging the challenges ahead but feeling ready to embrace them. "It's going to be intense," she admitted, "but I'm committed to both. I want to keep Harvest Creamery growing while I'm learning, and I know with you all here, we can make it happen." Her team nodded in support, each person eager to play their part in the next phase of her journey.

Riley thought about how far she had come. She remembered the early days at farmers' markets, where she'd handed out samples and explained her vision to every customer who stopped by. She thought about the support from her family and friends, the mentors who had guided her, and the community that had embraced her dream. Each step had been a testament to the people who had believed in her and to the strength she had found in herself.

Balancing university with her business would require focus and adaptability, but Riley knew she could handle it. She had always thrived on challenges, and now, with her team's support and her studies, she felt equipped to make her business even better. She was already envisioning ways to apply her coursework to Harvest Creamery, to refine her strategies, streamline her processes, and explore sustainable practices that could further distinguish her brand.

In her quieter moments, Riley reflected on the nickname "The Ice Cream Queen of Queens." She realized that it wasn't just about her—it was about the pride her community felt in seeing one of their own achieve success. Queens had been there for her, had celebrated her victories, and now, they were part of the legacy she was building. She wanted to give back, to show her gratitude, and to create opportunities for others, just as she had been given.

Looking ahead, Riley imagined expanding Harvest Creamery to new cities and connecting with farmers across the country. She could see the potential for partnerships that would bring her farm-to-table philosophy to new places, each one inspired by the local ingredients and traditions that made each region unique. She envisioned opening an online store, allowing customers across the nation to experience her flavors from the comfort of their homes. But she remained cautious, knowing that every decision had to honor the values that had brought her here.

Harvest Creamery wasn't just a brand; it was a reflection of Riley's heart, her dedication, and her commitment to community. As she prepared for university, she knew that her studies would only deepen her connection to her business, allowing her to bring fresh insights and innovative ideas to her team. She saw herself as both a student and an entrepreneur, learning and growing in both worlds, each one informing and enhancing the other.

When she thought about the future, she felt an overwhelming sense of purpose. She knew there would be long nights and challenges ahead, but with her team at Harvest Creamery and her new university path, she felt more prepared than ever. She was committed to her brand, to her education, and to the mission she had set for herself. Each day was a step forward, a chance to build on what she had created and to honor the support that had lifted her.

Conclusion: Lessons Learned

As Riley looked back on her journey from a 15-year-old with a simple idea to a successful entrepreneur and philanthropist, she felt an overwhelming sense of gratitude and personal growth. Her story was filled with challenges, triumphs, and invaluable lessons, each shaping her approach to business, life, and her relationships with others. These lessons went beyond profit margins and business decisions—they became guiding principles that would carry her forward in every chapter of her life. She knew that these insights, earned through experience, would continue to inform her future, both as the visionary behind Harvest Creamery and as a person committed to making a positive impact on the world.

1. Stay True to Your Values:
From day one, Riley knew that Harvest Creamery would be built on values she held close: quality, sustainability, and authenticity. Her dedication to ethically sourced ingredients and supporting local farms didn't just build a brand; it built trust. Each decision she made aligned with these core values, reminding her that success meant little if it came at the cost of integrity. As Harvest Creamery expanded, her commitment to these values only deepened, grounding her in a purpose that resonated with her customers and community. Staying true to her values was more than a business strategy—it was the heart of her journey.

2. Embrace Resilience and Perseverance:
Building a business from the ground up was an incredible undertaking, and Riley learned early on that resilience was essential. There were days when challenges felt insurmountable: when suppliers canceled, recipes failed, and she doubted her ability to succeed. But every setback taught her the power of perseverance. She realized that resilience wasn't about avoiding failure but about rising each time she stumbled, learning from every obstacle, and continuing to move forward. These experiences taught her that growth often comes from the toughest moments, shaping her into a stronger, more capable leader.

3. Seek Help and Build a Support Network:
Riley's journey was never one she walked alone, and one of her greatest lessons was understanding the value of support. Her parents, friends, mentors, and community all played a role in helping her navigate the complexities of her business. She learned that reaching out for help was a sign of strength, not weakness, and that a trusted network could offer guidance, comfort, and perspective when she needed it most.

She came to treasure the relationships she built along the way, realizing that success was not a solo endeavor but a shared accomplishment shaped by those who believed in her.

4. Hold Integrity as Your Compass:
As her business grew, Riley faced opportunities and challenges that tested her commitment to integrity. She learned that integrity was about consistency in her principles and staying honest and transparent, even when it was difficult. She realized that integrity wasn't just about how she presented herself publicly but also about the everyday decisions that kept her aligned with her values. Her commitment to honesty, authenticity, and ethical practices became her compass, guiding her through moments of doubt and reminding her of the kind of business—and person—she wanted to be.

5. Find Strength in Faith:
Throughout her journey, Riley discovered that faith—both in herself and in something greater—was a steadying force. Whether it was faith in her vision, her abilities, or in the goodness of the people around her, this inner trust allowed her to keep moving forward. She came to see that faith wasn't about certainty; it was about believing in her purpose, even when the path wasn't clear. In moments of self-doubt or challenge, her faith provided the strength she needed to persevere, teaching her that sometimes, trusting the process was the bravest choice she could make.

6. Continue Learning and Growing:
The decision to attend university while running Harvest Creamery was a testament to Riley's commitment to lifelong learning. She recognized that there was always more to learn and that her education could help her business flourish. Her university experience brought her fresh perspectives, new knowledge, and a network of professors and peers who broadened her horizons. Riley understood that growth required curiosity, adaptability, and a willingness to embrace change. She saw education as an investment not just in her business but in herself, a way to continually evolve and bring the best of herself to every endeavor.

7. Balance Ambition with Gratitude:
Driven and ambitious, Riley worked tirelessly to expand her business.

But she also learned the importance of gratitude, of pausing to appreciate the support, encouragement, and trust her community had given her. This sense of gratitude kept her grounded, reminding her that every achievement was a shared success. As Harvest Creamery continued to grow, she knew that balancing ambition with gratitude was essential to keeping her business meaningful and authentic. By remembering where she started and the people who helped her along the way, she stayed connected to her roots, knowing that gratitude was as powerful as any success.

8. Give Back to Those Who Helped You:
Riley's journey taught her that true success was measured not by profits but by the difference she made in others' lives. One of the most fulfilling aspects of her work was her ability to give back to her community and support others on their own paths. Establishing a foundation to mentor young entrepreneurs and support educational initiatives became her way of paying forward the support she had received. Her commitment to giving back wasn't just a gesture—it was a guiding principle, reminding her that her success could create opportunities for others to pursue their dreams.

9. Keep Your Vision Alive, But Stay Flexible:
From the beginning, Riley had a clear vision for Harvest Creamery, but she quickly learned the importance of flexibility. Adapting to challenges, evolving with customer feedback, and remaining open to new opportunities allowed her business to grow in unexpected ways. Flexibility became one of her greatest assets, enabling her to innovate and expand while staying true to her original dream. She realized that her vision didn't have to be rigid—it could evolve with her, shaping Harvest Creamery's future in ways she hadn't imagined.

As Riley stood at the threshold of her next chapter, she felt a profound sense of purpose. She would continue balancing university with her growing business, each enriching the other. These lessons weren't just for her business—they were lessons for life, reminders of what truly mattered. She was proud of the journey she had walked, the people she had met, and the brand she had built. Harvest Creamery was more than a business; it was a reflection of her journey, her values, and her love for her community.

She knew that these lessons—about faith, integrity, resilience, and gratitude—would guide her through every challenge and triumph to come. They were a part of her story, shaping the kind of leader, entrepreneur, and person she aspired to be. As she looked toward the future, she felt ready to continue growing, learning, and sharing her journey with others. The end of this chapter was only the beginning, and she was excited to see where her path would lead.

The End

Made in the USA
Middletown, DE
09 February 2025

70609931R00060